As I Remember

Lakeside Reflections of Mary Gilson Ferguson

Teri Ferguson Thompson

Teri Ferguson Thompson

Beaver's Pond Press, Inc.
Edina, Minnesota

ISBN 1-931646-96-1

Library of Congress Catalog Number: 2002115499

Book design and typesetting: Mori Studio

Printed in the United States of America

First Printing: November 2002

07 06 05 04 03   6 5 4 3 2 1

Beaver's Pond Press, Inc.   7104 Ohms Lane, Suite 216
Edina, MN 55439
(952) 829-8818
www.BeaversPondPress.com

To order, visit *MidwestBookHouse.com* or call
1-877-430-0044. Quantity discounts available.

This book is dedicated to
Jim Ferguson,
a loving son and father.

Contents

Acknowledgements

My sincere thanks and gratitude to the following people who made this book possible:

Cindy Rogers, for her expertise as an editor.

Milt Adams at Beaver's Pond Press, for his kind and gentle mentoring.

Jaana-Maria Bykonich and Jack Caravela, the design team at Mori Studio, for making the book look so good and for their incredible patience dealing with a novice, such as myself.

My brother Randy Ferguson, for his proofreading skills, his great suggestions and our late night phone discussions.

My dad, for furnishing the historical pictures of Randolph, for sparking my interest in genealogy, for being a saver, and for taking me on my first train ride.

Julie Buehler, for being my best friend.

Lew Linde, a messenger sent by God. He was a total stranger who walked into my life in the summer of 2001 and told me exactly what I needed to hear. He spoke the right words at the right time, giving me permission, in a sense, to begin my journey writing this book.

Randy, my husband, and my children, Matthew and Kelsey, for fending for themselves far more than they cared to over the last fifteen months.

All my family, for the love, support and encouragement they have always shown me, and for believing in me.

Lastly, Grandma, for her honesty and openness; for giving me something to write about. Without her, there would be no book.

Foreword

At the time of this writing, I have lived half as long as my grandmother. Of the forty-four years I've been in her life, she has been telling me stories of her past—bits and pieces here and there. The first forty-four years of her life, before I was born, were the ones that especially intrigued me, years I wanted to know more about. Those were the years that truly shaped the character of Mary Gilson Ferguson, the soft spoken, yet at times outspoken, humorous, interesting woman I know as my grandma.

So instead of just listening to her stories and thinking I would remember the details of her accounts, I decided to make time in my busy life to sit down with her, to really listen, to ask questions and to write it all down.

It amazes me how she can readily recall the address of where she lived eighty years ago and how much a loaf of bread cost in 1925, but she has trouble remembering what she did the day before yesterday, what she's suppose to do tomorrow, or where she put her grocery list. Ask a question about a person, place or thing in her life fifty years ago, and she goes back to it immediately. I can see it in her eyes, in her expression. It's as though she's viewing an inner screen playing the movie of her early life. She sees the characters, remembers the scenes and knows the dialogue. She is in the front row and she invites me to sit beside her as she narrates. Together we have the best seats in the house. We laugh at the funny parts, cry at the sad parts and applaud at the end. I give it an Oscar nomination.

Grandma and I sat out on her patio awhile back, admiring both the gorgeous weather of that summer morning and the beautiful view of the cliffs across the lake. After all these years she never tires of the view and neither do I. She told me she's getting old and wondering when the good Lord is going to take her. She complained how she didn't feel well the day before. When she had gone to bed that night, so tired and stiff, she prayed she would just go in peace and not wake up. I asked her not to say any more prayers like that because we had a book to write, so she promised me she'll hang on.

Even though I physically wrote this book, my grandma is the real author. Much of what you read is written exactly the way she told me, word for word. Some of it she even wrote herself in a red, spiral bound notebook she bought at the Dollar Store. We may have some dates mixed up, some facts and figures incorrect, and we may have offended or slighted someone, none of which is intentional. This book is my grandma's perception of the way things were, mixed in with some facts I researched, so if there is disagreement with either my grandma's perception or the accuracy of my research, so be it and we apologize.

In my many visits and conversations with my grandmother I grew to know her better, understand her more clearly, and love her more dearly. We've formed an unbreakable bond and a wonderful friendship. I've been fortunate to have this relationship with her. It's been a learning experience and a gift I will forever be grateful for.

*O*ne

Grandma Garth wasn't really my grandma, but I called her that just the same. Rosie Garth was a widow in our neighborhood who enjoyed my visits. I remember, at age three, walking across the dead end street we lived on to get to her house. When I arrived at her doorstep, she would exclaim, "My you've had a long trip. You must be tired." "Yes, I am," I'd tell her. She always put two wooden chairs together for me to lay down on. The hardness was uncomfortable, so it wasn't long before I would tell her I wasn't tired anymore. Then she fed me cookies.

The town of Clarion, my birthplace, is in central Iowa, about twenty miles west of Interstate 35.

Birthplace, Clarion, Iowa

Back in 1914, the year I was born, there were no four-lane highways—just bumpy, dirt roads and lots of wide open space to swallow up the dust.

I often took my little tin pail down into the ditch right next to our house, to get dirt to play with. The ditch was all that separated our house from the railroad tracks, which were the interstates of that time.

My father, Guy Gilson, worked for the Chicago Great Western Railroad as a carpenter. His job involved lots of traveling to make repairs on the railroad's bridges, water towers and depots. He worked six days a week, coming home Saturday nights and going back on Sunday nights. He had a lean build, a gentle smile, and worked like a dog to feed us ugly kids. I loved my father but we never saw much of him. It was my mother who was always there and did everything for us.

Born Lena Mae Bayles, my mother was a strong, capable, take-charge kind of a woman. She was bright and witty and ran the household with love and efficiency. Anything she decided to do was just fine with my father—he rarely questioned her. Before she met my father she was attending college to become a nurse, but quit her training to tend to her ailing mother. My Grandma Bayles was only 47 years old when she died in the spring of 1904. Why my mother

DEATH OF ANNiE BERRY BAYLES.

Passes Away After A Lingering Illness With Consumption. The Funeral.

Wednesday morning at three o'clock occurred the death of Mrs. Annie Berry Bayles at her home in Tippecanoe township, after a lingering illness with consumption. She was the wife of Benjamin Bayles and was about forty years of age. She is survived by her husband, one son and two daughters. Mrs. Bayles was a good woman and highly esteemed by all in the community, where her loss will be keenly felt.

The funeral services were held this afternoon at her late home conducted by Rev. Johnathan Lee of Vega.

April 27, 1904.

Rome, Iowa
boarding house;
Guy Gilson,
3rd from the left.

Guy and Lena's
wedding picture,
Aug. 30, 1905.

Lena's
wedding portrait.

didn't return to her schooling,
I never knew. She was cooking
and running a boarding house
in Rome, Iowa, when she met
my father. He and his younger
brother Frank ran a saw mill in
Rome. Late in the summer of
1905, Guy and Lena were married. According to my Grandma
Gilson's diary, they lived in Oakland Mills a few years, then
back to Rome for about a year, and then on to Clarion in

1910. Uncle Frank was working on the railroad there and probably enticed his brother to follow suit.

World War I broke out while we lived in Clarion. My father heard certain things were going to start being rationed, so he brought home a hundred pounds of sugar. Uncle Frank told my mother to get rid of it; they could get in trouble for hoarding. She had my father take it back to the store.

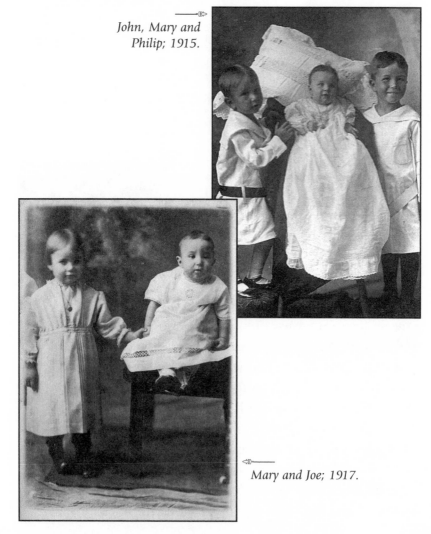

*John, Mary and
Philip; 1915.*

Mary and Joe; 1917.

My father was transferred to Kenyon, Minnesota, in 1918, when I was just four years old. We first rented a house near Main Street but were only there a short time, maybe a month, before we moved to the edge of town into a large, spacious house—fourteen rooms in all—that we rented from Dr. Hewitt. Here we had a big yard, a barn, and a few outbuildings, like my mother wanted, where she could keep some animals, and keep us kids off the street. She bought a milk cow, a hog and some chickens to raise. She also planted a huge garden, so we ate well. My mother was a wonderful cook, never skimping on rich ingredients such as her hand-churned butter and fresh cream. She made the best pancakes I've ever eaten in all my years. She was always busy but never complained.

I had two older brothers, Philip, the oldest, and John, next in line. Then there was me and last, my younger brother,

John, Joe, Lena, Guy, Mary and Phil.

Phil, Joe, Mary and John.

Joe. We all had certain chores around the house to help out Mother. She worked so hard to keep us fed and healthy. One of my chores was to go over to the Gundersons who lived just across the street and get the table scraps they saved for us to feed to our hogs and chickens. Mr. Gunderson owned the flour mill down by the tracks. They lived in a big, beautiful house which is now a historical site in Kenyon. I'm sure they were the richest family in town at that time. So I would go with my pail to the back door to collect the "goods." One day when I went over, no one answered at the back door, so I went around to the front and knocked. Hattie, the oldest of the three daughters came to the door. She had never married, so was considered an old maid. I looked up, smiled and said, "I came to get the slop." She glared down at me and spoke through gritted teeth, "Don't ever come to this front door and ask for anything like that again." I turned and ran home crying, feeling like her words slapped me in the face. I begged my mother to never send me there again. I'm not sure who took over that chore—maybe one of my brothers, but I never had to go back.

The Hewitt House, as we called it, was chilly in the winters. There was a hot air furnace in the old, dirt-floored basement, but just one register came up into the dining room. The front room was closed off in the cold months, as were some of the rooms on the second level. The dining room doubled as a sitting room during those times. The cook stove in the kitchen was the warmest spot in that big, old house. The summer kitchen, which was just off the main kitchen wasn't used in the winter either, of course. Come warm weather again, we would spread out into the expanse of our big house.

Paved streets were unheard of in those days and transportation was mostly horse and buggy. Very few people owned automobiles. Fewer yet flew in airplanes. Seldom did we see a plane, but when we heard one, someone would holler in excitement, "airplane!" and everyone would come out of their houses and look up to the sky in awe. We never had a car or horse and buggy to take to town. When we needed groceries, my mother called in the order to be delivered. We didn't buy much from the grocer since we raised so much of our own food.

Every Sunday we walked to the Methodist Church which wasn't too far from our house. The walk to school was about a mile, but it seemed ten times that, especially in the winter when the snow was above my knees. No one shoveled their sidewalks, if there were any, in those days. I was so tired by the time I got to school, I just wanted to sleep. That's probably why I never learned much.

I loved playing with the Hanson kids who lived in a nice, big house across the road. Rueben Hanson, their father, was

Mary holding the little boy who lived upstairs.

Charles and Sadie Larson.

the mortician in Kenyon. He had five children and we always
had a lot of fun together.

My mother rented out part of the upstairs to various
boarders. I remember a young couple who rented from us
one summer. I played with their two small children. There
was a stairway on the outside of the house that led up to the
second floor, so the renters had their own entrance.

Then my father's cousin, Sarah Larson, and her invalid
son Emery came to live upstairs. Before they moved to
Kenyon to live with us, Cousin Sadie, as we always called her,
had lived on a farm near Lockridge, Iowa, with her husband
Charles. After he died, she rented the farm out and moved to
a small house close by to my Uncle Orson and Aunt Mary's
farm in Oakland Mills. Aunt Mary, for whom I was named,
was my mother's younger and only sister.

Once, when we were visiting Uncle Orson and Aunt Mary,
my father called on his cousin Sadie and witnessed the run-
down conditions she and Emery were living in. He also discovered the renters she had on her farm were taking advantage of
her by not paying the rent and ruining the land. My father told
Sadie that if she would deed her farm to him, he would take
her and her son back to Minnesota with us and take care of
them. Sadie was in agreement with that, so the legal arrangements were made and back to Kenyon we all went.

What my father didn't know, at the time, was that along
with the farm he inherited hundreds of dollars worth of
debt—lumber bills and other expenses. And my mother inherited more work, for the family expansion was quite a burden.

Emery was a big, strong fellow, in his late twenties, when
he came to live with us. He had attended college and Sadie
was so proud of him. At some point in his young adult life,
he had been stricken with polio. The disease had left him

unable to walk or talk. Vaccinations for polio didn't begin until the mid 1950s, so back in the early 1900s the infectious disease was widespread in our country. I always felt sorry for poor, tiny Sadie, burdened with this great big, grunting son.

We children had our rooms upstairs and Sadie and Emery shared a bedroom up there also. They even slept in the same bed; she never left his side. Mother brought up their meals three times a day. There was no bathroom in the house, but we had a chemical toilet upstairs. So there they stayed. As time went on, Emery's care became too much for his aging mother, so he was put in the State Hospital in Rochester. Committing him was so hard for Sadie; she cried often. My mother took her to see him now and then, but it was a chore to do so. First she had to find someone to look after us kids. She and Sadie would then take the early morning train from Kenyon up to Randolph, wait for the Doodle Bug, which was a one car passenger train that took them over to Red Wing, and then finally down to Rochester. They only had a short time with Emery and then the trip was reversed. They wouldn't arrive home until late in the evening.

The conditions that Emery was subjected to were very upsetting to my mother and Sadie, but it was what had to be done. Emery died a year later and Cousin Sadie went on to live with us for many years.

$\mathcal{T}wo$

In 1925, much of my father's work was in St. Paul, so my parents made the decision to move there in order for him to be home more evenings. Mother had an auction in Kenyon and sold most of her household furniture, since the row house we were moving to in St. Paul was furnished. The prospect of a new place sounded exciting, but I soon missed our big yard in Kenyon.

Our new residence at 552 Dayton Avenue was in a beautiful, three story, brick and stone building, which consisted of five dwellings, side by side, each with an identical front door and large stoop. The row house was built in 1889 and still stands today in all its glory and grand, architectural design. The basement, where our family's bedrooms were, was partially finished off. It was cheery compared to some of that time, since the windows were good sized and allowed plenty of natural light to come in. The kitchen, dining room and living quarters were on the main floor. Bedrooms and a bathroom on both the second and third floors were where the tenants slept. This was the first house I lived in that had indoor plumbing, which was a real luxury for us.

My mother took in roomers and boarders in order to make some extra money. She charged $7 a week for a room, which included breakfast and

Joe and Mary.

552 Dayton Ave, St. Paul.

supper Monday through Friday. No meals were served on the weekend. Although she was a good business woman, she lost money because her rates were low and she fed her tenants so well. Everyone loved Lena's delicious cooking and generosity.

My job was to set the table, help serve the food, and assist with the clean up. When Mother called in an order to

Schock's Meat and Grocery, she sent me on the trolley car down to Seven Corners to pick it up. Seven Corners was a busy place with all the streetcars, buses, and autos coming in. I walked a few blocks to Dale to catch the streetcar. In those days we bought 10 tokens for a quarter. I was able to use just one token for the round trip by getting a transfer ticket once I got off at Seven Corners. For the return trip I used my transfer on the Selby car which took me back up the hill toward home. The Selby Avenue Tunnel was the most fun. The streetcar's lights came on as we entered the darkness. I enjoyed all the sites and sounds of the city. The trolley's conductor was a nice man. He helped me on with my two heavy bags of groceries. I suppose he thought it a big load for a scrawny eleven-year-old. I always felt safe and was used to traveling in the streetcars by myself.

Little did I know that in the mid 1920s, St. Paul was in the midst of a crime wave, one of the worst in its history. Prohibition, which began in 1919, played a large role in the heavy crime. Gangs, bootlegging, gambling, prostitution and violence were rampant. Establishments, where they sold the illegal drinks, were called speakeasies. Many of these places opened up around Seven Corners. The Brown Derby was a popular spot of the times. I've heard that St. Paul saw the likes of Dillinger, Ma Barker and her boys and many other notorious gangsters. I, of course, was oblivious to it at the time and thankfully unharmed by it all.

From where we lived, it was just a short walk to Webster School. I had only been in the sixth grade for one month when I came down with a bad cold, a sore throat and the most swollen glands a person could imagine. I couldn't even turn my head; it looked like grapefruits on both sides of my neck, resting on my shoulders. I was so very sick that all I could do was lay in bed. My mother applied scalding hot poultices to my bulging neck in hopes of drawing out the infection. One side broke in the night and oozed out onto my pillow, leaving me in a lopsided state. As a result, I had neck problems for years. My condition worsened as more symptoms appeared; an uncomfortable rash and a dangerously high temperature. I had scarlet fever. It was as though my strength and my thoughts were being burned out of me. I couldn't stand even the slightest noise and I lost all my hair. I think I had a nervous breakdown of some sort. My mother, who had scarlet fever herself but never let on, did her best to nurse me back to health. She should have been in bed and quarantined too, but she went right on cooking, serving meals and washing bedding for her tenants and the rest of the family.

My mother never took us to conventional doctors. If she couldn't come up with an effective treatment from her doctor's book, or a natural home remedy, she called upon a faith healer. The big, fat 'Divine Healer Lady' had her office in St. Paul, where we usually saw her. But in cases like mine, when someone was too sick to leave their bed, she made house calls. It was $1.00 for a treatment. She came and shut her eyes, laying her hands on different parts of my head and body and called forth her healing powers. I'm sure she was a fraud and it's a wonder I didn't die. Many children did die in those days of diseases like scarlet fever and rheumatic fever.

I don't remember a Christmas that year. I don't remember much of anything as time and memory faded to a blur and I lay in my basement bedroom. Forty-nine pounds, weak and pale, I finally emerged from my sick bed late that following spring. I had missed an entire school year and months of my childhood, but I survived scarlet fever and so did my mother.

To further recover from my illness and get a little color back into my cheeks, my mother thought the fresh air and sunshine of an Iowa farm would do me wonders. That summer she put me on a train to Aunt Mary's house, along with my brother Philip. He went down every summer to help Uncle Orson on the farm. I didn't protest about going, but once there I was so homesick. I really just wanted to be back home with my mother. There wasn't much excitement on the farm. Aunt Mary and Uncle Orson were busy people, working hard all day long trying to make a living, taking time out only to go to church on Sundays.

Aunt Mary was a good person, but she wasn't used to having children around, since she was never able to have any of

Aunt Mary, Mary and Phil, ready for church.

Aunt Alta and Uncle Philip.

her own. She had a particular way of doing a job and liked things just so.

Aunt Alta was different. She was married to my mother's only brother, Philip Bayles, for whom my oldest brother was named after. I spent one week with them and it was the best week of the whole summer. They lived on a farm at the top of

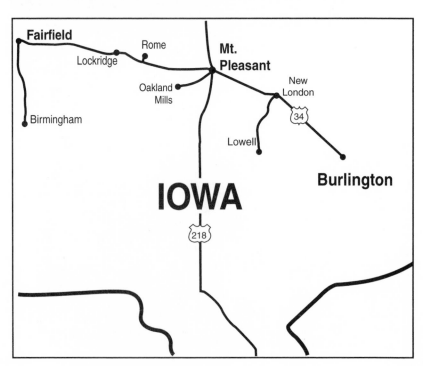

a hill looking down on the little town of Lowel, Iowa, which was about twenty miles from Uncle Orson's farm. Even though it wasn't far by today's standards, then it was quite a long trip up and down the dusty, bumpy roads in the old Ford. Cars in those days didn't go too fast and especially on terrain such as that.

Like Aunt Mary and Uncle Orson, Aunt Alta and Uncle Philip never had any children, either. I had no cousins on either side of the family. My father's only surviving sibling, his brother Frank, never married. There had been a brother, George, who died at just ten months of age, before my father was born. His little sister Lizzie died when she was only four years old.

My Grandma Gilson wrote this heartbreaking piece in her diary sometime after her daughter's death in 1878.

> *My sweet little girl. My baby. She was but 4 years and one month old. When like a dew drop, she went to the warm sun. Yet she left my heart as I have seen ground left out of which a storm had torn a great tree. Oh, child of my heart. I can feel thy soft kiss on my lips just now, and would give all I have for one look of thy dreamy eyes. But I cannot have it. Yet we are taught that God is love. But thy death makes me wonder and cry in pain. Baby, baby. I could begin the world again without a laugh or a friend, if I had but thee. Such beginning with all its hardships would be welcome misery. I do not wonder that the grass is green and soft that covers your little grave. And that the summer birds sing their tender notes as they sit on the branches of the trees. My God, Father of mine in the blue Heavens, is not this the heaviest cross that can crush the weakness of my soul? Yet that green grave, not four feet long, is where I*

*Rebecca Gilson
with daughter
Elizabeth.*

*love to linger, and where I pray, and say strange words.
Baby I am coming, coming soon. Do you see me? Will
you know me? Oh, baby. Sweet baby. I will try for your
sake to be a better woman. But, oh my darling, my own
dear child, my heart sobs and breaks.*

My mother thought she might be childless like her siblings,
since she had been married five years and still was not pregnant. She went to a doctor in Keokuk, Iowa who performed
some sort of surgery, which proved to be successful as it
enabled her to have four healthy children. She used to tease
that it was the dumbest thing she ever did, having that surgery.

Aunt Alta let me be myself. She let me help her with the
dishes and didn't scold me or correct me on the way I did
things. She let things go and had some fun. The neighbor
children were invited over and we turned somersaults out in
the yard and made her laugh. She was never much of a
housekeeper. She'd hit the high spots and let the rest go.

Alta, Philip and Orson one Sunday afternoon

Uncle Philip had a deep raspy voice, just perfect for calling out the square dancing when he played his fiddle on Saturday nights down in Lowel. One time when Uncle Philip was ready to go to town, he sat in the car and honked his horn for Aunt Alta. He always did this when they were going somewhere and his impatience drove Alta crazy, just as her slowness at

Uncle Frank, Uncle Orson and Phil, harvest 1924.

getting ready drove him crazy. So on this particular day, she was still in the tub when she heard the honking. She came outside, dripping wet and naked, with her arms in the air and yelled, "Do you want me to go with you like this?" When they told that story, it was always good for a laugh.

Uncle Philip loved his cats and worshipped his dog. They had a big, shepherd dog that I enjoyed playing with the summer I stayed there. His companionship helped me to forget my homesickness. He was a smart dog, too. Once Aunt Alta got stuck in the basement. The old cellar's trap door must have fallen shut and she couldn't push it open. She went to the small window and there was her trusty dog. She hollered through the glass, "I'm in trouble. Go get Philip." Off he went to the barn to get my uncle's attention. Then back he ran to the basement window where my aunt would encourage him again, "Go get Philip." Back and forth it went until my uncle thought it odd and followed the dog to the cellar window where he discovered what the commotion was about.

After my stay with the Bayles', it was back to Aunt Mary's for the rest of the summer. Poor Aunt Mary seemed unhappy with her lot in life, especially as the years went on. She was a college graduate from the University of Missouri and was teaching school when she met Orson Milner. Once married, she had to quit her job, for in those days they only allowed single women to teach. It was a lonely life on the farm with no children. She spent most of her married life taking in and caring for sick, old relatives. She cared for her husband's Aunt Melissa until she died. Then she took care of her father-in-law, who was blind. I remember getting a horse and buggy ride from him when I was little. Even though he couldn't see, the horse knew the way around the place.

Aunt Mary's own father, my grandpa Benjamin Bayles, who was getting up there in years and needed care, lived with

Aunt Mary off and on for a number of years. He was a gentle, quiet old man. It was said that he was part Native American, but I never knew. Whenever we would ask my mother what nationality we were, she would always tell us, "blue-bellied Yankees!"

Grandma Bayles had died years before so Grandpa Bayles had no one but his children. He lived thirty-two years beyond his wife. In those days, relatives took the elderly in, instead of putting them in a nursing home like they sometimes do now. He lived with his daughter Mary for six months and then with his son Philip for six months. I remember we took care of him one winter, but it was a long way for him to travel in his old age.

As time went on, Aunt Mary stopped smiling and became distant. Something was definitely wrong. I didn't know then about depression but I'm sure that's what she suffered from. Uncle Orson must have known his wife wasn't in her right state of mind, for he had a lady stay with her during the day while he was busy with his farm work. On a September day, in 1937, while her husband was busy out in the fields and

The Milner house.

the lady staying with them was busy tending to chores, Aunt Mary mixed herself an afternoon cocktail. Drinking Lewis Lye water was a painful way to leave this world. It burned her insides something awful from her mouth all the way down and she suffered terribly. My mother and brother John, who were then living in Iowa, were called to her bedside. It was so very hard on my mother to watch her sister die like that.

Three

In the fall of 1926, I repeated the sixth grade since I had been sick the year before with scarlet fever and missed so much school. While my brother and I had been in Iowa for the summer, my family had moved from the row house to a smaller house on Pleasant Avenue where the rent was cheaper, so I was now a student at Jefferson School. Two of the boarders followed us in the move. Both were nice, old gentlemen who loved my mother's cooking and gladly continued paying for room and board.

We lived near the St. Paul Cathedral and I remember one time going to church with a friend there. My mother had given me a dime for the collection dish, so when we entered the magnificent structure I saw a large vessel of water and put my dime in it. I thought it much like a wishing well and wondered why no one else was putting their coins in the lovely bowl. I wonder who fished out my dime from the Holy water that day. Although we had attended Sunday school and church regularly when we lived in Kenyon and my mother was a member of the Ladies Aide there, we never went to church while we lived in St. Paul. I'm not sure why.

My mother made most of my clothes when I was little. She bought flour in 100 pound sacks and made curtains and nightgowns from the printed cloth. We were fussy about picking out just the right sack of flour. It had to have a pretty design on it. As I got into the upper grades, she hired a seamstress to make my dresses. Even though money was always tight, Mother made sure I had a few nice things to wear. I usually got one new dress in the fall, made of a heavier material to keep me warm through the winter months. I always changed into old clothes the minute I got home from school. That way my new dress wouldn't need to be washed as often and would last longer.

In February, 1927 we moved from the hustle and bustle of city life to Randolph, a small town about thirty miles south. The railroad transferred my father there, where he had a little workshop across from the depot. His monthly earnings at that time were around $150.

The Hotel Randolph was run by Mr. and Mrs. Peters, who also owned a house a block or so from their hotel. Their son

DEPOT&ELEVATORS, RANDOLPH, MINN. 11

had been living in the house, but had recently moved out and it was now for sale. Prior to his transfer, my father had learned that the Peters were looking for a buyer for their house on the hill. It was a good sized place with a barn, out buildings, and a large yard; and it was close to the railroad depot. The Peters' house sounded perfect for us. The purchase price was $7,000. At age 57, my father began making monthly payments on our first home.

Randolph was a railroad town and the majority of its residents worked for the railroad. The busy terminal was a stopping point for a number of trains coming from all directions. The Chicago Great Western had its mainline running from the Twin Cities through Randolph to Chicago. If I remember right, there were about twelve passenger trains that came through town each day. Trains from Kansas City, Chicago and

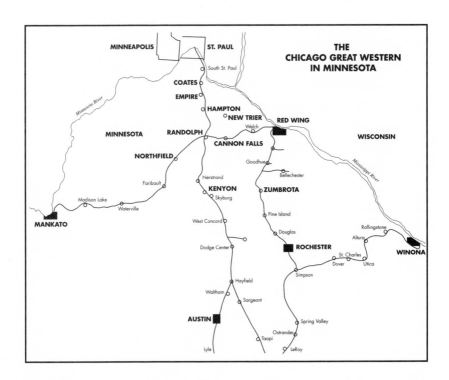

Omaha would pass through on their way to Minneapolis and St. Paul's Union Depots.

My dad never owned a car and there really was no need for one. We walked where we needed to go in town and because my father worked for the railroad, our family had a pass to ride the train anytime we needed to. The trains were comfortable with their nice, upholstered seats. The cars were heated in the winter, but in the summer it could get uncomfortable. Air conditioning was non-existent at that time and the cars would get very hot and stuffy. We could open the windows for fresh air but then we had to put up with the cinders flying in our face. In those days the trains were pulled by steam engines. Later, in the mid-forties, they modernized to diesel engines.

The railroad companies had their ups and downs over the years. Around the turn of the century there was much competition between the different companies to buy up land, build new mainlines, and secure freight and passenger business. Miles of track were laid across Minnesota and around the country in a very short time. An economic slump occurred from 1910 up until April of 1917, when the U.S. declared war on Germany and World War 1 began. Many of the railroads filed bankruptcy during that time, but after the war things began to look up. The 1920s were considered the "Golden Era" of railroading.

During this time, Randolph saw lots of business. The Red Bird was a fast new train, painted a vermillion red with gold wheel spokes. The striping and lettering were all painted in gold also. It was always polished to a high shine. It provided a two-hour and twenty minute, non-stop run from St. Paul to Rochester, via Dodge Center. It did occasionally stop in Kenyon for water and passengers were allowed to board there. With the Mayo Clinic's growing reputation for quality medical services, this was a popular train. I never rode on the

Red Bird; we didn't have passes for the fancy trains, but I saw it pass by many times.

The Blue Bird was another fancy train I never rode on but admired just the same. It, too, traveled from the Twin Cities to Rochester, stopping just three blocks from the Mayo Clinic. Along the way it made stops at Randolph, Cannon Falls, Red Wing, Goodhue, Zumbrota and Pine Island. It was designed to boost passenger business which was on the decline in 1929, because people were beginning to buy automobiles. The Blue Bird had three coach cars, the first of which was decorated in shades of blue, with deep plush seats and wide aisles. The exterior was painted a rich blue with lettering in gold. It was advertised as,

> ...*gas-electric powered, smokeless, spotless, cinder less. It has a parlor-observation section, and buffet services at any hour and a complete Pullman section and coach car, all scrupulously clean.*

My brothers, Phil and John, were going to Mechanic Arts School in St. Paul at the time of our move to Randolph and wanted to finish out the school year there. Early every morning about 6:00 they took the train into St. Paul and walked from the depot to school. They got home at night around 5:30, just in time to eat supper. No doubt they were hungry. The next school year for Phil was spent in Iowa. After working on Uncle Orson's farm, as he did each summer, he decided to stay on and attended school in Mount Pleasant. He graduated from there in 1928 and continued living with my aunt and uncle, farming full-time.

I remember the first day of school at Randolph. Joe and I didn't know anybody as we stood under the big clock in the hallway, watching all the unfamiliar faces. Joe leaned into me and said, "Let's go home and get Ma."

Randolph Consolidated School.

"No, Joe," I assured him. "We'll stick it out." A teacher finally spotted us and took us under her wing. Kids can be cruel to the new kid in town. Because of the swollen glands I had with scarlet fever, I always had neck problems and held my head kind of awkward. Some of the kids at school called me "stiff neck." That hurt me more than my neck.

The first school bus.

We enjoyed living in our new house in Randolph. It was wonderful to have a big yard again. I had missed that in St. Paul. There we had been more or less confined indoors, but now we could have our school friends come over to play and our country friends could spend the night, which happened now and then. I remember one time there was quite a blizzard and the horse drawn buses couldn't get the country kids home, so there were about a half dozen kids that stayed overnight that evening.

Our new home also had plenty of room for animals and a garden again. My mother kept a cow for milking, a hog or two, a calf for butchering, and lots of chickens. The cow provided us with plenty of fresh milk. We had a big crock we dumped each pail of milk into. A piece of cheesecloth over the top strained out any foreign matter, such as straw or whatever might accidentally end up in the bucket. The crock was placed in a cool area—the back porch in the winter and the basement in the summer. We had to stir the milk with a big wooden spoon so the cream wouldn't separate. That was the whole milk we used for baking and drinking. Oh, how my brother Joe loved milk. He drank one glassful after another. If we wanted cream for coffee and for churning into butter, we let the milk sit without stirring it until the cream separated and rose to the top to be skimmed off with a ladle. My father always liked cream on his oatmeal. The remainder was the skimmed milk which we fed to the hogs and the cats.

At one time we had as many as twenty-three cats. Mother would go outside and bang her fist against the old tin pan and fill it up with milk. The cats knew what the familiar sound meant and they would drop from the trees, come running from the barn or dash out from one of their many favorite hiding places. It was quite a sight to see them all gather for their milky treat.

The Gilson house.

Lena Gilson.

Mary and her cat Murca.

My mother usually planted two or three gardens. We ate lots of fresh, home-grown vegetables in the summer. She planted plenty so she could can some to be enjoyed during the long, cold winter months. She canned lots of green beans and they were so delicious. Her secret touch was to put a slice of fried bacon in each jar for flavor.

On Sundays we always had a big chicken dinner. Mom went out in the yard with her chicken catcher, which was a stick with a stiff, wire hook on the end that she could grab the chicken's legs with and pull it in close so she could get a firm grip around its neck. She put an end to the chicken's life one of two ways. Either she laid its neck in the special spot by the chicken coop where there was two nails spaced apart just so, on a wood stump, and off went its head with a sharp little axe. The other method was to wring its neck. She twisted and turned and yanked it around until the body fell off. It would flop around quite a bit at first. I suppose if any of my grandchildren or great grandchildren, none of whom were raised on a farm, were to witness something like that now, they would think it was just horrible and never eat chicken again. But when a person grows up seeing that kind of a thing, you think nothing of it.

So the chicken would be left to lay there until it bled thoroughly. Nowadays it seems they don't do this properly, with their quick process of killing chickens assembly-line-style. The bones are always dark, which is proof they don't let them bleed long enough. Back then, after dinner, you had a plate full of nice white bones. Once the chicken had bled sufficiently, Mom put it in a pot of boiling water to scald it and then we picked off the feathers. This I often helped her with. Once plucked and clean, she cut it up, dipped it in some seasoned flour and fried it up in some sizzling lard in her big cast iron skillet. Along with the delicious chicken, we'd have mashed potatoes, gravy, vegetables and bread—everything farm fresh and home-grown. Sometimes friends from Kenyon were invited up for Sunday dinner.

Every dish my mother made was good. She had a cookbook but I never saw her open it. I remember tasty hot dishes made with home-made noodles. For dessert she made mouthwatering pies, such as rhubarb or pumpkin, topped with fresh whipped cream. We always ate well. Her baked beans were a favorite in the neighborhood. The kids would say "Mrs. Gilson's making beans!" But that was one dish I hated.

Because we didn't have a refrigerator, there was no way to keep leftovers, so we ate what was cooked and each meal was started from scratch.

In the summer we bought our beef and pork at Ohs Brothers Store. Frank and Charlie Ohs ran the general store in town. They sold just about anything there—from groceries to hardware and even ladies nylon hosiery. There was a big walk-in cooler in the back where they stored all their meat. Since we had no refrigeration at home, we fattened up the hog and calf all summer long and butchered in the early winter. Mother canned some of the meat and the rest she wrapped in paper and kept on the cold porch or in a snow bank where it could freeze. Our neighbor, George Hagen (he was a railroad man, too), got all his meat stolen one winter.

Ohs Brothers Store.

Ohs Brothers Store.

It was sitting under a tub out in a snow bank in his yard, easy access for a hungry thief.

The hams were cured with salt and hung in the attic of the house, where it was cold in the winter months. If the pork wasn't properly cured—not enough salt or smoke—insects would lay eggs in the flesh. I remember one time when my mother went up to the attic to check on the hams, she found them spoiled, full of little maggots. We had to throw them all out. All that hard work for nothing.

Joe and I walked home from school every noon for our lunch. My mother always had a nice hot meal for us. A dish we always enjoyed was the morning's leftover oatmeal mixed with a beaten egg and enough flour to make a firm patty. Mom fried the patty in bacon grease and topped it with maple syrup. Once I got home from school in the afternoon, it was my job to do up the lunch dishes, which I hated doing. They were always there waiting for me, but it was the least I could do to help out. My mother was busy out in the garden hoeing or hanging out laundry or a number of other chores she did without complaining.

Another chore I had was to deliver the chickens my mother cleaned, or dressed as she called it, for the railroad dining car. I brought them down to Jeff, the cook on the dining car, everyday and sold them for fifty cents a chicken.

We had lots of chickens, so therefore lots of eggs. I brought them down to Ohs Store to trade for groceries or other supplies. We got about twelve cents a dozen for them. Another smaller grocery store in town, Miller's Store, was owned and operated by Louie Miller. That's where the Randolph Post Office was, too, in a little space in his store. Back then it cost two cents to mail a letter. Behind the store, in the alley, was where Louie kept the empty butter crocks. In those days people bought butter by the crock and then would return the empty crock to be used again. There was a five cent returnable deposit. Sometimes I would walk through the alley, pick up an empty crock, go around to the front, walk in and get five cents for it. I never got caught, but I didn't do it too often.

Right across the street from Miller's was the bank and next to that was a tavern and restaurant that changed hands many times. When we first moved there, I think it was Schulers who ran it. Across the main street from the tavern was Doc Peter's Drug Store. It was more a men's hangout than a drug store and I'm not sure what kind of prescriptions he filled, as Doc Peter was a veterinarian. Ed Brown had an auto repair shop right next to the drug store, which he rented out from Dickmans and down from that was Hedke's Blacksmith shop. Up the hill behind Main Street, by the grain elevator, was the fire station and next to it was Lambert's Lumber yard. Most of the buildings were built of wood, rather than brick like some of the bigger towns. All the streets were unpaved. Randolph was a humble looking community.

Randolph, 1920s.

Four

When I was about thirteen years old, life didn't seem so bad. No one had money but we were all in the same boat so it didn't seem to matter. We weren't envious of anyone because no one had anything to be envious of. I always had enough to eat, a warm place to sleep, clean clothes to wear and a family who loved me.

The hotel ran a contest once, with a box camera as the winning prize. Whoever had the most candy bar wrappers could be its owner. Every time I got a nickel I bought a candy bar and other kids gave me their wrappers, too. Not many people had cameras back then, so I felt pretty lucky walking out of the hotel with my shiny, new one.

We had our innocent, childhood fun. There were two water-filled gravel pits in town, simply called the 1st pit and the 2nd pit. The 2nd pit was also known as Cordes' pit, since it was on the land Mr. Cordes had bought after the Randolph Sand and Gravel Company had abandoned the sights. In the winter we skated at the 1st pit. Our ice skates clamped on to our shoes in those days. We would be half froze but that didn't keep us from going back the next day. In the summer, we trekked out to the 2nd pit to swim. It was a long walk for us, as it was on the far end of town from our house. It seemed even farther on the return trip home after wearing ourselves out swimming and being in the sun all afternoon. It's no wonder I was so skinny.

I remember my first kiss from a handsome young boy named Donald Palmquist. I really liked him and he used to come over to play cards with my brothers and me. One night we were sitting out on the front porch and he leaned over and kissed me. Then he ran home as fast as he could. My folks never liked him because they said he was too mouthy. He just liked to talk a lot, was all. That never bothered me. One day he and his mother moved and that was the last I saw of Donald.

I took piano lessons from Celia Miller, Louie Miller's daughter. I wasn't too interested in the whole thing, but Mom thought I had talent, which I didn't. My brother John was the real pianist in the family. When we had taken piano lessons in Kenyon from Mrs. Leland, John had caught on to it much better than I. He even played in a program at church one time. Phil used to play the violin and Joe, well…he just played hooky. Clair Morrill and I once performed a duet on the piano at school in Randolph when Miss Haglund was the music teacher.

We had many good teachers at school. Our high school principal was Eva Bradford. She was also our English teacher. Our school day started off in Assembly, with Miss Bradford sitting up front at her desk. We all paid attention to her. She had a stern, but friendly, manner about her. She never had to raise her voice; she just had a certain way of looking at us and we knew we had to listen. During assembly, all grades— eight through twelve—gathered in the large room on the second floor. After attendance we began our English lessons. Then we dispersed to our separate classes such as chemistry, algebra, sewing and history. Our history teacher was Miss Ida

Mary Gilson, top row, second from left.

Snyder. She was also a good teacher, but she had no discipline over us and we treated her badly.

School ate up most of the hours of a weekday, but we made time to go to the movies now and then. Billy Morrill, who lived on Lake Byllesby about a mile out of town, always walked to school. As he passed my place I would join up and walk along with him. He used to take me to the Grand Theater in Northfield when we could find a ride, since Billy didn't have a car himself. It was 25 cents to get into the show, but we never got popcorn because we couldn't afford it. Sometimes Lyle Miller took us in his car. Billy would walk to my house and Lyle picked us up there, then he headed toward Northfield. His girlfriend, Erlis Melby, lived on the way there, so she got picked up last.

One particular evening, Lyle had a bottle of liquor with him. When Erlis got in the car she could smell it on his breath. She wasn't too pleased and let him know how she felt about it all. We still took in the show, but when it was time to go home, Erlis wouldn't get in the car with Lyle. I finally said, "Oh Erlis, just get in and I'll sit in the front with Lyle. We have to get home." So she got in the back with Billy and I sat in the front. Just outside of Northfield, without any warning, Lyle pulled off on a back road in a wooded area and stopped the car. Erlis was even more perturbed at him now. She wanted out and for some reason Billy followed her. There I was alone in the front seat with this brute. All of a sudden he started pawing at me like some disgusting animal. I got away from him and out of the car, but he was out just as fast and threw me down on the ground, his heavy weight on top of me. I yelled for Billy, and thank God, he was there in no time and pulled Lyle off . I was so shaken, I'll never forget it. Billy, Erlis and I got in the back and Lyle took us all home. We never asked him for a ride to the movies again.

When I was a bit older, fifteen or sixteen, we'd have some fun on a summer's evening going up to Coates Dance Pavilion. Coates wasn't much of a town with its one little grocery store, but the dance hall was the town's attraction and all we cared about. My brother John would drive a carload of us in his Overland, with its cloth top and no windows. It was a great fifteen-mile trip in an open car.

Once to our destination, we paid the twenty-five cent cover charge and kicked up our heels to the tunes of Whoopy John's orchestra. We waltzed and fox-trotted into the night, working up quite a sweat on the dance floor. On the trip back home, the dust rolled in off the gravel roads, choking our laughter and sticking to our tired, perspiring bodies like a second skin. Such a good time it was.

In the late 20s the fashion industry came out with—what they called—street pajamas, a one piece pants outfit. Up until that time, girls always wore dresses, but when the new fad came out, I just had to have them. I remember I got some blue ones. I wore a lot of blue because I was told it brought out the blue in my eyes. I also remember the look on my dad's face when he saw me in my new attire. He said, "Don't let me catch you going up town with those pajamas on." But of course when he wasn't looking I was up town.

My father was from the old school where women wore dresses and didn't cut their hair. He certainly didn't approve when my mother got her hair cut into a stylish bob. When I got my first permanent wave he didn't say anything, but gave me a sour look.

Getting a perm in those days was quite a procedure and sometimes risky. The permanent wave machines were a contraption, to say the least. The thing loomed over one's head like an octopus with many rope-like arms. At the end of every "arm" was a metal clamp which was attached to each perm rod, so there a person sat with this monster affixed to her scalp. Mom and I sometimes went to a beauty school in St. Paul where they offered their services at a low cost. One time, my mother went there to get a curly do, and ended up with a bad burn on her neck. The hot steam from the perm machine had scalded her. She screamed out and the gals all came running to attend to her. They felt so bad and fussed over her, applying salve to her tender, pink skin.

To get our hair to keep a nice finger wave, we went to the grain elevator and bought a handful of flax seed for a nickel, carrying it home in a little paper bag. We boiled the tiny seeds in water until a thick, slimy mixture was created. We put the home-made setting gel into our hair, placing in the waves just so with our fingers, then sat out in the sunshine to dry.

I always enjoyed our trips to St. Paul. Once a month my mother and I took the 35 to 40 minute train ride uptown. Just going to the St. Paul Union Depot was a treat in itself. It's a beautiful building with so much grand space for the eyes to admire. A person was always on duty with a rag, busy polishing the fine woodwork. There were many rows of benches to sit on while waiting for a train to come in. They were made of rich, smooth wood and the man in charge of polishing them would politely ask the mothers to keep their children's feet off the seats. A nice dining room and a fancy gift shop were open along the perimeter. Even the restrooms were elegant. The depot was a busy place with all the comings and goings of the trains and its passengers. It saw millions of people come through its doors each year. In fact, its doors are still open today, although not to train travelers. There are a few restaurants and shops inside, along with it's timeless beauty.

Sometimes my good friend, Florence McEathron, and I went shopping if we got a little bit of spending money, which wasn't too often. Even when we didn't have any money, it was still fun to window shop in St. Paul. Her dad was a railroad man like my dad, so she had a free pass to ride the train also. We shopped at the Golden Rule and The Emporium on 7th Street, which were department stores of that time. Sometimes we went to Montgomery Ward, a big beautiful store, which was out a ways but worth the extra walk. If we were lucky, we might have enough money to buy a hamburger or something at Grants, downtown.

If we were in need of a notebook for school, we made sure it had a red cover. When our faces needed a little color, we tore a small piece off the front, moistened it with our spit and rubbed it on our cheeks. We always applied our "rouge" once we got to school so as not to be seen by our mothers. One time, I must have overdid it a bit and the teacher made me go wash my face. I don't remember her name but I remember I never liked her.

Florence and I also liked to go to Red Wing on the Doodle Bug on Saturdays. The Doodle Bug was just a little one-car train and only held about fifteen to twenty passengers at a time. It went to Rochester and back everyday but Sundays. The Doodle Bug was the only train that occupied Randolph's small roundhouse each night. We'd go as far as Red Wing and get off at the nice, fancy depot there. As we walked to the other side of town we could see our destination looming large above us; Barn Bluff. We took all day climbing the huge scenic bluff, loving the freedom and fresh air. Once to the top we were like giants looking down over the town and the Mississippi River below. We could see for miles and miles. As if that wasn't enough walking, at the end of the day we hiked back to the depot to catch the evening train home to Randolph. To this day, people still enjoy the hiking adventures on Barn Bluff. They can even go to the depot, although they won't be able to catch a train there any longer. The building has been restored and converted into a Hardee's fast food restaurant.

I remember one Saturday's shopping trip Florence and I planned that almost didn't happen. That Friday, I left school and headed home for lunch as usual, happy that in just a few more hours another week of reading and arithmetic would be over. I could hardly wait for the next day's excursion to St. Paul, but at the moment I had to wait for the train that blocked my way. A person would often be held up on one side of the track or the other, while cars were hitched up or taken off or the Y track was adjusted, changing the course of the train's route. I had waited many times before, but on this particular hot day, I felt hungry, anxious and daring. I was only yards from my house, but this big, sleeping monster was in my way. If it didn't move soon, I'd have no time to eat and would be late getting back to class. The space under the box-car looked so inviting. One quick duck under and I could be on the other side, free to run home. I knew I could do it. It would only take a second to scoot under there. I had been schooled on the dangers of such things and the voice of my father's preaching entered my mind, but I didn't listen. I looked around. No one was in sight. Quickly, I crouched down and under I went. It surprised me how much farther it was to the other side and how time tends to stand still just a bit when your heart is pounding so hard. Just as the last of me came out from under, the train lunged forward. The steel of the wheels against the steel of the tracks could have easily sliced off my foot, but I was lucky that day. Scared to death, I ran home, but told no one about the close call.

The next morning finally arrived and I woke up early, excited. When I sat down to breakfast, my father informed me there would be no shopping for me that day. The conductor had seen my stunt and told my father all about it. I cried and begged and promised I would never, ever try anything like that again. My father, angry as he was, softened to my tears and let me go as planned. I was true to my word and stayed out from under trains after that.

A few times a year I took the long train ride to Iowa to see my Uncle Frank. He was still working for the railroad and had moved to Council Bluffs, which is near Omaha, Nebraska. Uncle Frank was a well-off bachelor who had

Uncle Frank.

plenty of money with which to spoil his young niece. He was always very generous with all us kids at Christmas time. Uncle Frank was fun to visit. He would meet me at the train station all dressed up in his fancy suit, looking very handsome and neatly put together. We ate in restaurants, which was something really special since I never got to do that back home. Uncle Frank stayed in a rooming house, but it didn't include meals like the one my mother used to run, so he ate all his meals out.

On one particular visit, however, Uncle Frank was a little late in meeting me, which was very unlike him. He looked somewhat rumpled, red-faced and glassy eyed, talking louder than usual. I didn't quite know what was up, but the visit was fun just the same. When I returned home, and my parents asked about the trip and Uncle Frank, I told them fine, except for the peculiar way my uncle had looked and acted. They didn't let on to me, but they suspected he'd been tipping the bottle and that was the last time they sent me alone to visit Uncle Frank.

He came to live with us the following winter and stayed for about nine months to recuperate. I learned later that Uncle Frank had a lady friend and they were going to be married. Things didn't work out between them, she got a hold of his money and ran off and left him. He began drinking heavily after that and fell into a depression. The country itself was in a depression, which caused Uncle Frank to lose his good paying job on the railroad. With no money, no job and no love in his life, he must have felt life wasn't worth it any longer. Mother asked if we ever wondered why Uncle Frank wore long sleeved shirts even in the hot summertime. He didn't want us kids to see the scars on his wrists. After his stay with us, he returned to Council Bluffs. He found work again, but never did get married. He died in Iowa in 1940 at the age of 59.

Five

The second summer we lived in Randolph, when I was fourteen years old, I thought it was time for me to go out in the world and earn some money. When I told my friend Florence about my bright idea, she got an even brighter one. That's how things worked with Florence and me. She was planning to go help her aunt for the summer. She had heard about a lady that lived near her aunt's house who was sick in bed and in need of some help. I could be that help! So Florence and I set off one morning, in the direction of her aunt and uncle's farm. We walked down a dusty, gravel road south of town, across the old steel bridge that hung over the Cannon River, and on another three miles. When we got as far as her Aunt's home, we said our goodbyes and I continued up the road a bit until I came to Mr. and Mrs. Ed Vanderhauvel's place. It seemed like a nice enough house and Mrs. Vanderhauvel seemed like a nice enough lady. I explained how I had heard she wasn't well and maybe could use some help around the house. She asked if I could hoe and weed the garden, cook the meals, clean the house and tend to the baby and their three-year-old daughter. With an air of confidence, I assured her I could. But really I didn't have much experience with any of those things. She asked me how much money I thought my services were worth. I said, "Oh, $2.50 to $3.00 a week." In my mind, I was hoping for the $3.00, of course. She seemed anxious to have some help and said that would be fine.

I hurried home to pack my bags, this time making the hot, dusty trip back to town without the companionship of my friend. Mr. Vanderhauvel was to come for me later that day. When I told my mother about the arrangements I had made, she didn't exactly share in the excitement over my new job. She reluctantly let me go, figuring I'd be home the next day, I'm sure.

The first night was awful. I was given the little bedroom off the kitchen and it seemed strange to be sleeping in a different bed. I was homesick right away and missed my mother and the crisp, clean sheets of my own bed. Then, to make matters worse, a huge bat swooped into my room. I was petrified and called out Ed's name but no one heard me. I pulled the dirty bedding up over my head and cried myself to sleep, lonely and scared. I was determined to stick it out and never let my mother know how homesick I was.

Ed had milk cows. One cow in particular, a stubborn, red cow, always kicked as he milked her. He called her "the old red bitch." One hot day, as I was hoeing the garden, the little girl was beside me pulling up the vegetables instead of the weeds. When I told her to stop, she said, "No I won't, you old red bitch."

I managed to somehow stick it out for a week when Mrs. Vanderhauvel said I could go back home. I'm not sure if she was feeling better, or if my cooking and cleaning weren't up to snuff, or maybe they just couldn't afford me any longer. No matter the reason, I was glad to be relieved of my duties. Apparently, when we were negotiating wages the week before,

Mrs. Vanderhauvel had the $2.50 in mind rather than the $3.00 like I had hoped. When it was time to pay me, she had only three ones and no change. She told me I could leave the fifty cents down at Ohs Store and the next time they were in town to get groceries they would pick it up there. So Ed brought me home in the old Ford. It was a wonderful feeling to be going home.

Well, I never did leave the fifty cents at Ohs Store. After all, that could buy a lot of candy and other necessities. A few days later, while I was in the store, I saw Mrs. Vanderhauvel. I quickly ducked behind some shelves stacked high with goods. I felt a bit guilty about the whole thing. I don't know if she saw me that day but I do know she never saw her fifty cents.

My mother was known to have quite a green thumb and a love for growing things. Not only did she have vegetable and flower gardens outside, but the inside of our home reflected her passion for gardening, also. On every window sill and sunny spot in the house were pots of green foliage and colorful blooms. One night my father was taking a bath upstairs when all of a sudden my mother heard him yell out, "Bring the plumber's friend!" What he meant was, "bring the plunger," but she didn't understand what he was saying, so she went upstairs to see what he wanted. When she opened the bathroom door she had to laugh at the sight. There was my father, sitting in the tub, amidst the African violets and begonias, which had fallen from their perch on the window sill above him. The water was murky with the potting soil

Lena and Guy.

and he was now dirtier than when he first stepped in for his bath. He had to laugh, too. I think humor was my parents key to a good relationship. Of course, my mother couldn't resist telling her friend, Helen Morrill, about the funny incident. After that, whenever Helen saw my dad she would tease, "Say Guy, have you taken any mud baths lately?"

Back in those days, people had cisterns to catch the rainwater. That was the best soft water for washing clothes and bathing. The gutters on the outside of the house ran down into the big cement cistern in our basement. My father wasn't a man to get riled or use cuss words, but one thing that brought out the anger—and thus, some swearing—was the chore of fixing the old cistern pump, which pumped the rainwater up to the kitchen and bathroom. It was old and the motor needed some tender, loving repairs now and again. I can remember us kids sitting around the kitchen table eating and Dad down in the cellar, banging around. Every once in while we heard a "damn it." My mother opened the stairway door and said, "Guy Gilson, you stop that swearing! We've got children up here."

The only other time I ever heard my dad swear was when I was twenty years old. That was the age I started the filthy habit of smoking cigarettes. All my friends were smoking. I thought if that's the thing to do, I better learn to do it. It seemed sophisticated and I didn't want to be left out. So I got dizzy and threw up, but I kept at it until I got the hang of smoking. Off brands were ten cents a pack and the popular ones like Pall Mall and Camels were fifteen or twenty cents. No filters, of course, and no talk of the dangers of it. My mother knew I smoked, but my dad didn't. One morning after breakfast, I went up to my room and cracked open the window to have a cigarette. After I came back down, my father went up to use the bathroom. As he passed my room, he couldn't help but smell what I'd been up to. When he returned to the kitchen he asked me if I smoked. I said I did.

"I'll be damned. I never thought I'd have a daughter that would smoke!" He shook his head as he walked out of the room. I felt so cheap.

My mom said, "Now you've done it. You ought to be ashamed of yourself." And I was. Not enough to make me quit, unfortunately.

Later, when my parents lived down on the farm, I used to go to the outhouse to smoke. My mother told me he said, "Why doesn't she just smoke in the house instead of freezing her butt off out there?" But, although I was a grown woman, I still was careful not to smoke around him. He would enjoy a cigar now and then, but he and my mother never smoked cigarettes. I went on to smoke for nearly fifty more years and now I puff on inhalers to help me breathe instead of puffing on Old Golds to make me feel cool.

My dad always had a very calm demeanor. Nothing shook him up too much. My mother once said to me, "You know, he could see the hearse come to pick up one of you kids and he wouldn't blink an eye." He never showed much emotion. They say a woman tends to marry a man much like her father. I did.

$\mathcal{S}$ix

One very hot and muggy day in 1930, Randolph was changed forever and the people living there at the time would never forget it. It was late in the afternoon on Friday June 13th, when my mother sent me on an errand to Ohs Store. On my way, I passed Dad's shop, so I stopped in to see if he wanted anything from the store. He didn't so I went on my way. What I bought that day, and what happened to it, I have no recollection, but the rest I remember as though it were yesterday.

On my way back from the store, the sky darkened and rain began to fall. Just about the time I was passing Ed Brown's repair garage on Main Street, it was really coming down. The big sliding door was open so I dashed inside the building to stay dry and wait it out. Ed and Bob Ferguson, a friend who helped out in the shop, came toward the open door where I was standing. I remember saying, "My, it's raining hard!" Just then a terrific wind rose up and right before our eyes a tree uprooted across the street in the Murrays' yard.

"Head for the basement!" Bob yelled. Not knowing the layout of the building, I followed him and Ed followed me. It wasn't much of a basement, just one small room. We had barely gotten to the first landing of the stairway when the whole building collapsed around us. We were trapped, unable to get

The repair garage where Ed, Bob and Mary were trapped. At Mary's feet, the window from which they escaped.

back up the stairs. Ed was frantic, repeating over and over, "Oh my wife, my baby." He was married to Florence's sister, Evelyn, and they had just had their first child.

Ed started pulling boards away, trying to find the small window that he knew was our only way out. Bob warned him to be careful, that "the whole thing could cave in on us." Ed finally cleared away enough rubble and lifted himself up, crawled out the window, and started to run home to see if his family was safe. Bob yelled at him to stop and come back. "We've got to get this girl out of here!" Ed pulled me out as Bob boosted me up from below.

I never did ask Bob how he got out that day, because Ed and I just left him there. That was the second time I met Bob, who was to be my future husband. Of course I didn't know that at the time. I only knew I must get to my family. I ran home as fast as I could, jumping over downed light poles and wires. Thinking back on it, it was a wonder I wasn't electrocuted. As I ran into our yard, my brother Joe jumped out the dining room bay window. I thought how odd and funny this was. I just wasn't comprehending what had happened.

Later, they told me how Joe had been outside before the tornado hit and when he attempted to come in the house, as

The Gilson house still stands (between elevator and water tower). Others weren't so lucky.

hard as he tried, he couldn't open the door. John tried to help from the inside and finally, mustering up all the strength they had, the two of them were able to fight the wind and get it open. Just as Joe got inside, all the west windows on the ground floor blew out and some upstairs on the east side, too. My mother looked out the window at one point, probably to see if my dad or I were in sight, and had actually seen a horse and wagon fly through the air. It was later found in a field northeast of town. It was all so surreal, for I had never even heard of a tornado. My mother, having lived in Missouri when she was younger, knew full well what tornadoes were and what damage they could do.

When it was over, John and I went in search of Dad. When we got to his workshop, we found nothing but a pile of wood. John started pulling away the boards from the flattened mess and suddenly stopped. There lay Dad's hat. "I can't look anymore," John said. We walked towards the elevator where we met a man and asked him if he had seen our dad. He said, "I think I am your dad!" He was so filthy black we didn't even recognize our own father.

He had seen the tornado coming and had told Fritz, the old fellow who flagged the crossing, to take cover. They lay down and held on to the strong steel of the railroad track, their bodies taking a beating as they hung on for dear life. My dad's skin and clothing, even his pockets were blown full of dirt and cinders. Old Fritz's appearance hadn't changed all that drastically. He didn't bathe too often and was covered with dirt most days anyway. But they were lucky to have escaped the ravaging winds of that tornado with only scrapes and bruises and dirt.

Walter Drappe, the section foreman on the railroad, wasn't so lucky. He was the one person killed in that storm and it's amazing there weren't more. He and his crew were coming in

Devastation at the railroad yards.

on their motor car when they saw the dark funnel cloud approaching. He told them all to lay down in the ditch, which they did, but as Walt lay there, the black swirling winds picked up a big boxcar off the tracks and threw it on him, cutting his body in two. Some of his crewmen were injured. Carl Holtzmer, who later became Florence McEathron's husband, and Helmer Nelson were two that I knew of that were hurt quite badly. Mr. And Mrs. Lewis Contell escaped injury, since they were down at their lake cottage at the time. Their house in town was completely demolished and their bathtub was found in a farm field near New Trier, about nine miles away. Other homes and businesses were lost. Miller's little store and post office was damaged beyond repair. Ohs Store was damaged some, but they were still able to carry on business without interruption. Doc Peter's place was totally wiped out, along with McClintock's Garage, Woodman Hall, the blacksmith shop and of course Dickman's Garage, where I had been.

Our family was more fortunate than some. Although we had some wind and rain damage, at least our house was still standing. The tornado had taken off the chimney so we weren't able to make any fires until that was repaired, but we were lucky to have a two burner kerosene stove to cook on. Most everyone had wood cook stoves in those days, and many lost their chimneys also, but unlike us, had no other means to make meals. The Red Cross came in and set up a portable kitchen and dining room in the school to house and feed people.

My mother lost a great many pullets in the storm. I remember her taking a bushel basket out and picking up all the dead chickens. There were white feathers everywhere, as if giant snowflakes had fallen in June.

The whole town was without electricity, of course, since the tornado had created a tangled mess of all the electrical poles. The National Guard was called in to help. The devastation was great and there was so much clean up to be done, but I'm sure all were thankful to still have their family and loved ones with them. This tornado hit during the early years of the depression when no one had much to begin with, but with what we had the town began to rebuild. For years my mother would never leave the house on Friday the 13th. Even now, whenever black clouds roll in and the familiar smell of a storm is in the air, I head for the basement, remembering and reliving that day—over seventy years ago—when nature's giant fury met up with an innocent, little town.

Joe on far right.

Main Street—left standing is Mrs. Dickman's house and the Wallace house; gone is Doc Peter's, the repair garage (where I was) and Hedke's Blacksmith Shop.

.

Seven

The very first time I saw Bob Ferguson was in the home of his parents, James and Kathryn. The Fergusons were railroad people also; Bob's dad was an engineer for the Chicago Great Western. They had moved to Randolph from Mankato in 1922. Their house was a block behind the hotel, not far from our place and I used to pal around with Bob's sister, Peggy. One day, Peggy and I and several others went over to her place. We walked in and there was Bob sitting in the easy chair, reading. He was born with a book in his hands. Peggy said, "Oh, this is my brother. We *think* he's married." Bob never even looked up to acknowledge us. I'm sure he didn't want to bother with the likes of us, a

bunch of giggly, fourteen and fifteen-year-old school girls. He was a grown man in his twenties.

Peggy Ferguson,
Elizabeth Rosing and
Mary Gilson.

Then of course, there was the second time I saw him, our
"whirlwind meeting," in the summer of 1930. The third time
was at Ed and Evelyn Brown's house in the winter of that
same year. Evelyn and I were friends and I used to go over to
her place to play cards. We played lots of 500 and whist in
those days, it was cheap entertainment and something to do.
Bob was renting a room from them at the time.

His parents had moved to Red Wing the year before and
he was no longer living with his wife, Ruth. I never knew any
details of Bob's marriage, nor any reasons why it came to an
end. Bob was a very private man, one of few words and no
show of emotions. I didn't ask questions because it wasn't
any of my business and it wasn't polite to pry. Even after we
were married I never asked any questions because I knew
there would be no answers. I do know he and Ruth Verner
were classmates in high school, both graduating from
Randolph in 1925. At some point Bob married Ruth and
moved to Minneapolis, working in St. Paul for a Buick dealer
by the name of Warren Given. He and Ruth had a son, born
April 12th, 1930, whom they named Robert. It seems he did-
n't spend a great deal of time with his new family, always
working and helping Ed out at the garage in Randolph,
which is what he was doing the day of the tornado. After that
building was lost in the storm, Frank Klar built an automo-
bile repair shop on the west end of town. So now Ed and
Bob were working together at Klar's Garage and Bob was living in Randolph again.

Just a fun little tidbit here about Ed Brown's mother. She
divorced Mr. Brown and later married Mr. Gray. She lived a
colorful life.

Many nights I bundled up and walked the few blocks to
Evelyn's for our foursome of cards. I never had any romantic

As I Remember

inclinations toward Bob at this time. After all, he was seven years older than I, a married man and a father. But as winter neared its end, a new romance would begin. One March evening, a month before my seventeenth birthday, Bob asked me if I would like to go to the movies in Northfield. I hesitated, for although I knew he wasn't seeing his wife, he *was* married. I was also very shy and leery of dating, not being able to forget the incident with Lyle Miller. But Bob was very much a gentleman, quiet and polite. It seemed harmless enough, I supposed, so I said I would like to but that I would meet him at Ed and Evelyn's and we could go from there. I thought it best he not come to the house.

After our first date he dropped me off by the back door and thanked me for going with him. Bob worked every other night, which meant he was free to take me to the show on the opposite nights. I was quite timid and worried if I was very good company. I never knew what to say. After a couple of weeks of movie-going, I was beginning to care for Bob and I could tell he had mutual feelings. One night, as we sat in his car, he reached over to get his hat from the back seat, leaned in a little closer and kissed me. I was startled and didn't say a word, but I was happy about it. I never encouraged him for any further kisses although I wanted to. My shyness held me back and so did Bob's I think , for it was quite awhile before the next kiss came.

After we had been acquainted for some time, I asked why it had taken so long for that second kiss. He thought I had been mad at him for the first one, taking my silence as an indication I didn't like that sort of affection. So he wasn't going to take any further chances.

I began to fall in love with this handsome gentleman. I knew I couldn't continue to sneak around behind my

Bob Ferguson.

mother's back; I felt too guilty keeping secrets from her. So I told Bob I must tell my mother about us. He felt sure, by doing so, our dating would be put to an end, but I knew I had to tell her. It was a sunny spring morning and Mom and I were having breakfast. John and Joe had just left for school and I was purposely hanging back so I could talk to her and come clean about what was really going on. I told her about the trips to the show house with Bob instead of playing cards or going out with Billy Morrill like I had lead her to believe. She didn't say much, only that we must tell my father. I begged her not to tell him but she said we must. Once he knew I was sure that would end everything.

I couldn't concentrate a bit on my school work that day. I was doing so poorly in school as it was and love in the air wasn't doing a thing to help the situation. I was already in the 9th grade for the second time and because I missed a year of school with scarlet fever, my younger brother Joe and I were now classmates. My friend Florence had quit school and was already married. All I could think about was how much I loved Bob and what my father was going to say and do about the whole thing when he found out. When I saw Bob again, I told him that if he wanted to go with me anymore, he would have to talk to my father.

That Sunday, my dad was out in the front yard trimming trees when Bob came over for a man-to-man talk. They knew each other already. Right after high school, Bob had worked for my father on the bridge gang. I was peering through the window as they stood outside and conversed. It seemed they talked forever. By the time Bob left and my father came into the house, I was a bundle of nerves. Bob had tried to persuade my father into letting us see each other. He explained that his marriage was basically over, although legally it wasn't, yet.

My father said I could not be alone in Bob's company because he didn't want his daughter getting involved in a possible divorce suit, which was likely to come. It was decided we could go to the movies only if we had a chaperone, so an arrangement was made with Christine Nelson, a married woman who lived in town, to accompany us on our dates. She was very obliging as this meant a free movie ticket and a chance out of the house for her. Although this wasn't ideally what we had in mind, we figured we had to make the best of it. So every other night the three of us were off to Northfield. I think Christine probably enjoyed those evenings more than Bob and I did.

I complained to my mother that this whole thing was getting expensive for Bob now that he had to buy three movie tickets just to take me out, so a new plan was devised. They said it would be okay if he came to the house to visit. Again, this was not exactly what I had hoped for but at least Christine was out of the picture.

Bob and I worked crossword puzzles together at the dining room table so we had a good excuse to sit close to each other. He usually stayed for dinner and loved my mother's cooking, as everyone did. My parents liked Bob. He was very much a gentleman and his politeness won them over. They

Bob, 1931.

Mary, 1931.

"The Point" on Lake Byllesby.

eventually started letting us take a drive, but only during the day and we were to be back before the sun set. We used to drive to nearby Lake Byllesby and found a secluded spot out on the point. It was a small peninsula that pushed its way out into the blue waters of the man-made lake. We sat beside each other on the shoreline and Bob used a stick to write "I love you" in the warm sand. I picked up my own stick and put a question mark at the end of his words. He brushed away the sand, erasing the question mark and all doubts in my mind by putting a period at the end, instead. This ritual repeated itself from time to time.

That summer of writing love letters in the sand was also the summer of clamming. It was 1931, when jobs were scarce and people did what they could to make some money. Bob, his younger brother Don, and my brother John set up a camp down by the Cannon River, on the outskirts west of town and hunted for clams. It was really a lovely place there by the water's edge, wooded and peaceful. They erected a big canvas tent which housed a makeshift table and their cots. It was homey in a sort of outdoorsy, rugged way.

They had a flat-bottom boat they walked along side as they followed the river's winding path in their high rubber boots. The boat pulled a bar that had ropes attached to it with big steel hooks on the end, which clawed into

Bob.

Bob and his stockpile.

the river bed, digging up the clams. At the end of a good day they returned to camp with a boat full of the river's treasures. The clams were unloaded and dumped into the cooker, which was a huge metal pot filled with water, perched over the open fire. The clams were boiled until the shells popped open. With a pitch fork, they threw the clams on a slanted table, which allowed the hot water to run off. Buckets of cold river water were thrown on the pile to cool them off quicker. When they were cool enough to handle, they pulled the meat from the shells and tossed the shells into a pile. Most of the discarded meats were given to local farmers for pig feed. The men tediously searched the slimy flesh for the lovely pearls. I went down there now and then and helped. I never could eat clams after those days.

Don found the biggest pearl that summer. The pearls were separated by size and put in glass jars. Sometimes they just found irregular pearls or broken pieces which were called slugs. A man drove up to Randolph from Reed's Landing once a month or so to buy the findings. He loaded up his truck and hauled away the shells to a factory to be made into pearl buttons. The pearls and slugs, he sold to a jeweler. I kept one perfect pearl and had it made into a beautiful ring, which I wore for years.

The three men camped there all summer long. They took turns cooking each day. Sometimes my mother cooked the guys some food and our neighbor would give us a ride over. I'm sure they enjoyed those delivered meals over their own concoctions.

While Don was frying pancakes one morning, John was preoccupied with his eyes glued to a book, as they often were. He didn't notice when Don dropped a pancake on the dirt floor of the tent. Don brushed it off as best he could and simply served it dirty side down. John had a peculiar habit of always looking under his food before he ate it. I don't know why, but he tended to do this and I saw him do it many times at home. Maybe it was just to see if the underside of whatever he was about to eat was done. So on this particular morning his plate was set before him, he put his book down, lifted the edge of his pancake to have his usual look and all hell broke loose. They really got into it and John declared he was going to kill Don. Bob had to get in between them and break it up.

On another occasion, when Don was cooking, John sat down and began to eat. He asked what he was eating. Don said, "Remember that dead pig we saw down by the river this morning..?" That's all it took; John immediately lost what he had just eaten. It's funny he ever trusted Don to cook for him again.

Others took up clamming also. Tony Kruze and his wife Sadie dug clams and would take them back to their place to find the pearls. By summer's end they had built up quite a stock pile of the opalescent shells, waiting for the buyer to come. One Sunday afternoon, they returned home to their whole pile gone. The long summer's hard work and sweat hadn't paid off a cent for them during those hard times.

Once more people got involved in clamming, there weren't many clams left to be found. By summer's end, the clamming business came to a close.

Bob's marriage also came to a close. His estranged wife had sued him for divorce more than once, and each time he made an effort to work things out. The attempts were probably just to keep his parents off his back. I think they were the force behind his returns to Ruth, and Bob wouldn't think of contradicting his father. They felt he had a moral obligation and a responsibility to fulfill, especially since there was a child involved. Bob was probably thinking of the financial aspect of it all. The one and only comment he ever made to me about his first wife was he couldn't afford to stay married to her. She had been an only child and was possibly used to getting what she wanted. Evidently she wanted many things and expected her husband to provide them for her. Although it would cost him money to stay married, a divorce would also empty his pocket book. Bob was very cautious in his spending habits. That's my polite way of saying he was tight. The hard times and his upbringing greatly influenced his view on money, which he maintained throughout his life. His parents were also extremely frugal and thrifty (more polite words for tight).

So Bob was sued for divorce once again, this time finally signing the legal papers. I'm not sure what he paid out as a settlement, if anything, but I know he was to pay $10 a month child support, which he did sporadically over the next several years. When he missed a couple of months in a row, the local constable contacted him, informing him he needed to pay or be put in jail. So Bob tried to catch up. Several years later, after Ruth and Bobby had moved out to Seattle and she had remarried, her lawyer sent papers for Bob to sign, giving up his parental rights so that his son could be adopted by Ruth's new husband. He signed the papers, never letting on how he felt about the whole thing.

The divorce made things much easier for us as a couple. We were free to see each other when and where we wanted to. Bob spent a lot of time at our house and my folks fell in love with him, too.

Bob + me.

$\mathcal{E}ight$

After graduating from Randolph High School in 1930, my brother John had taken odds and ends jobs whenever and wherever he could. He did some painting and papering, worked as a farmhand for local farmers, and got on with the railroad, plowing snow off the tracks in the winter. He eventually was hired full time with the Chicago Great Western, working under my dad on the bridge gang, for which my dad was still foreman. The bridge gang built and maintained the railroad bridges, and repaired the rails.

My mother also became an employee of the railroad in the early '30s. She was hired as the cook for the bridge gang. Dad's health was beginning to fail

Lena and Guy (center) with the bridge gang.

at this time. I'm not sure exactly what his ailments were, but I know he ate lots of garlic for stomach problems. He always had a distinct smell of garlic about him. My mother was glad to be with him all week so she could take care of him and cook him a special diet. Of course the bridge gang loved her cooking. Mom and Dad were gone all week long, working and living on the train, coming home only on the weekends.

John was gone a lot too, but came home a few nights during the week. During our childhood he and I were always battling. We could hardly look at each other and were constantly on the outs. One time I got so sick of his teasing I picked up an incense burner from the coffee table and threw it at him. It missed and broke a knick-knack of mother's. She was so mad at me. I never hated anyone more than I hated John. But now that we were a little older and Mom and Dad were gone so much, we had to stick together.

One day, while I was cleaning out the pantry, John offered to wipe the dishes for me. I thought, 'Boy, this is a change.' After that, we got along pretty well. I guess we finally grew up.

Joe and I were always pals. We now had the house to ourselves most of the time. I missed my mother's company during the week. Joe and I fended for ourselves, which we were certainly old enough to do, but it was much nicer when Mom was home, cooking and looking after us. Joe

Joe.

74

and I ate a lot of eggs and toast then. We had one of the modern conveniences known as the electric toaster. The only thing was, it didn't have the automatic pop-up feature like today's toasters. We had to watch it and manually pop it up when it was done to our liking. We often forgot and ended up burning more toast than we ate. When we finally got a pop-up toaster, we thought we had it made.

Those years in the thirties were so hot and dry. The history books refer to it as "the dust bowl years" and that describes it well. It just never rained. For a few summers we kept the storm windows on to keep out some of the dust, but they never fit real snug and the dust sifted in anyway. The gritty dirt sat a fourth inch thick on the window sills.

Joe and I were now in the 11th grade. When school started and we came home for lunch, I had to go out and water the chickens. We no longer had a cow, since my mother wasn't around to milk. Mr. Klein, the milkman, delivered our milk in glass bottles. So it was just the chickens I had to worry about. I felt so sorry for the poor things. There they would stand with their mouths open, waiting for their noon drink. I'd go into the little well house, pump water into a couple of pails and haul it out to the tin water troughs for the thirsty chickens. I usually grabbed a quick sandwich, and then took a hot walk back to school.

It was 1932 and I didn't find my junior year to be any easier or more pleasant than the previous school years. I remember sitting by the window in Assembly, hoping to catch a glimpse of Bob. From my perch I could see Klar's Garage where he worked. Every once in awhile I spied him walking around, going about his business, not knowing I was up on the second floor of the school building, daydreaming about him. I wanted to quit school, but my mother wouldn't hear of it. She said I would go until I was thirty if I had to. So I stayed in school but dreamed of the day when I would be done and free to do as I pleased. I fantasized about someday marrying Bob and having a little place of our own.

Franklin D. Roosevelt became president that year while the country was in the midst of what would later be termed as The Great Depression. It was a terrible time. Millions of people suffered in poverty in those years, and hundreds of thousands were jobless and homeless. I've read that farmers dumped out milk and killed baby pigs to drive up prices, while people starved in the cities. We were luckier than the city folks, because we could at least raise our own food and we weren't going to bed hungry.

The railroads were in danger of going bankrupt and a third of the workforce was laid off. Those that still had jobs were forced to take a cut in wages and reduced working hours. One Christmas, my Dad was laid off. Things were pretty tight during the holidays that year. My only present was a ten cent ink tablet. Ink paper was smooth and much nicer than the rough paper of a pencil tablet. The gift still didn't seem like much but I knew things were rough and we were lucky to have a roof over our heads. Thankfully, my dad wasn't laid off for long. We were fortunate he had a good job to go back to.

It was during one of those hot summers of the dust bowl years, July of 1932, (before Mom started working on the railroad), when tumbleweeds rolled outside and the air in the house was as heavy and still as the dust on the sills, that my father's cousin Sadie was nearing her eightieth year. Old Sadie had been living with us for the past nine years. She slept in a tiny bedroom upstairs and because of her failing health, she could no longer make it down to the kitchen. Mom brought meals up to her and used her good nursing skills to make Sadie as comfortable as possible. But there wasn't much comfort in the heat of that summer, especially on the second floor of our house. One day, Mom and I were helping her into the bathroom, and she was feeling very poorly. Although she was just a little thing, we were having trouble handling her. She had no strength left of her own. We called my dad up and he helped us get her back to her bedroom. She was embarrassed that Guy saw her without clothes, but that's the only way she could bear the heat during the day. Once back in her room, she collapsed onto the bed and breathed in the room's stifling air for the last time.

My mother covered her body and I ran to the hotel to call the morgue. They came with a stretcher and as they took her down the slant of the stairs, her bodily fluids made a trail down the steps and out the door. I grabbed a bucket and a rag and washed up the mess. I didn't realize that happened when a person dies. It was the first time I had seen someone's life end and the memory isn't pleasant. A few days later, my mother went on the train to Iowa with Sadie's body and had her laid to rest. I remember standing in the yard crying as my mother left. Poor, old Sadie.

$\mathcal{N}ine$

In the spring of '33, my brother John put in a huge planting of potatoes. I spent many hours picking potato bugs off the plants, dropping the pesky beetles in a can of kerosene I carried with me up and down the rows. By late July, the potatoes were ready to dig, so Joe and I got the bright idea we would try and sell them to the local store owners to make some money. We dug many a potato and lugged our harvest around from place to place trying to sell our dirty load. I felt like we were a couple of gypsies, Joe and I. Each time, we returned home with just as many potatoes as we had started out with. So much for bright ideas of making money. A friend of Bob's later told us how his family ate nothing but potatoes, three times a day. It's all they had and they fixed them every way possible—fried, baked, mashed but it was still just potatoes all the same.

I filled in as the bridge gang cook to give my mom a week's vacation during that summer. She enjoyed her much deserved time off and spent one day of it on a shopping spree in St. Paul. She bought a beautiful couch and chair with green upholstery and some other nice furniture. The money my mother earned was spent on the house and us kids.

I'm sure the guys from the railroad were glad to see Lena return. My cooking wasn't anything like my mother's, but I managed and they survived.

Toward summer's end, my mother arranged a wonderful trip for Joe and me. A man that worked on the railroad had told Mom how his wife and young son were going to go stay with his sister-in-law in Chicago and visit the World's Fair. His wife's sister had a basement apartment she rented out to teachers during the school year, but it was now vacant for the summer. My mother worked it out so that Joe and I could go with this man's wife and stay in her sister's little apartment. She paid for our lodging and gave us some spending money, even during those tough times. At least our train ride was free.

We left on a Monday night and arrived in Chicago on Tuesday morning. We were so excited to be going somewhere and doing something. We visited Lincoln Park and that evening took a bus tour around the big, lit up city of Chicago. We spent the next three days at the magnificent World's Fair. Admission was fifty cents and for a quarter, I bought a souvenir book telling all about the fair. The fair was spectacular and futuristic. Some described it as "modern" or "dazzling." It certainly was all that. There was the Island Midway, with lagoons on one side and Lake Michigan on the other. The Enchanted Island was great fun with its games, shows and rides. The Sky Ride was being compared to the Eiffel Tower. From a couple hundred feet above, we could see all of downtown Chicago and even across the lake to Michigan. The World's Fair was a great success, even though—because of the depression—it was a low time in people's lives. I suppose people could go and forget their worries for a short time. It seemed we were in another world, being in the midst of the lights and color and magnificence of it all. For two poor kids like us, it was a dream come true.

Joe and I had a great time, except that Joe had just gotten a new pair of shoes and his poor feet were so sore the whole trip. On Friday evening we left for Randolph, saying good-bye to the Windy City. It was uncomfortably hot returning by train, but we had wonderful memories of the fair to keep our minds off of our discomfort. And Joe didn't have to walk on his blistered feet any longer. Miss Florence Haglund, the music teacher from school, was on the train ride home. She'd been at the fair also. We got back to Randolph on Saturday morning to find my brother Phil, his new wife Carolyn and their two-week-old son Franklin at our house. That's when things went from really good to really bad.

Phil had been living in Iowa for the previous four years with Uncle Orson and Aunt Mary, working for them on their farm. Things were going fine until he got himself in trouble with an under-aged girl. It was quite an embarrassment for my aunt and uncle. The Milners were well-respected, church-goers of their tiny farm community, after all. Carolyn was pregnant and her family insisted Phil do the right thing by marrying her. So he did and brought his new bride home to the farm. It wasn't long before she was trying to take over and have things her way. I'm not sure what all went on there but I know there was a lot of tension between Aunt Mary and Carolyn. I think the final straw for Aunt Mary was finding the beautiful baby quilt, she had hand-stitched for the expectant couple, shoved under a pile of wood near the cook stove.

MISS CAROLYN BROWN AND PHILIP GILSON MARRIED SATURDAY

At the pleasant country home of Mr. and Mrs. Howard Brown southwest of Oakland Mills, a beautiful home wedding was solemnized Saturday at noon when their daughter, Carolyn D. Brown and Philip F. Gilson were united in marriage. Rev. Thomas Brown, pastor of Cedar Friends church, officiated. To the beautiful strains of Mendelssohn's Wedding March, played by Mrs. Bert A. Jay of Mt. Pleasant, Rev. Thomas Brown using the beautiful and impressive single ring ceremony joined these worthy young people in marriage. Only near relatives and friends of the two families were in attendance. A very pleasant and memorable feature was that the date, Jan. 14, was the birthday anniversary of both bride and bridegroom. These worthy young people are well and favorably known and have many relatives and friends who extend sincere congratulations. Following the ceremony an excellent four course luncheon was served. The color scheme of blue and gold was carried out throughout the rooms, the dining room and parlor being beautifully draped in these appropriate colors.

The bride's dress was of gold crepe, while the bridegroom wore the conventional suit of black. They will reside on the farm south of Oakland Mills. This immediate neighborhood has long been their home. These worthy young people have the sincere congratulations of all.

So they came to our house to live. I had never met Carolyn before, but the minute I stepped into the house I knew things were different. All our family pictures that had sat on top of the piano were gone, and in their place sat all of her family pictures. It wasn't long before she was telling Joe and me what to do and making our lives miserable. Carolyn, now eighteen, was older than Joe by just a year and actually younger than me, but that didn't stop her from acting like the head of the house and treating me like nothing more than the hired girl. Joe and I were starving by the time we got home from school at 4:00 in the afternoon and we were used to helping ourselves to a snack, but now we weren't allowed to eat anything until supper and that wasn't served until Phil got there.

He had found work as a farmhand and didn't get home sometimes until 8:00 at night. Joe and I had been used to being independent and doing as we pleased and now we had

Carolyn to contend with. She was ornery as hell to Joe and me but sweet as pie to John when he was around and lovely company when my folks were home on the weekends. Because they weren't at home all week, they didn't see first-hand what was happening to our once happy household. Carolyn manipulated and lied to them all. She questioned what Bob and I were up to the evenings we went out. She told many lies, one of which was that I had spit on the baby. I couldn't believe she could make up such a thing and even more upsetting was the fact that the rest of them believed her for a time. I loved little Franklin; he was a sweet, innocent child. It was his mother that I would have loved to spit on. It seemed as though she was trying to turn my family against me. I was doing very poorly in school—my senior year—and I was a total wreck. I decided I had had enough.

I'd heard about a lady who might need some help in her home. Mrs. Alma Siewert was in her early forties and pregnant with her first child. She and her husband lived out in the country a ways, with no phone. One day I had Bob take me out to their place and explained my awful situation at home. I told her I desperately needed to get out of my house and offered to help her out in exchange for room and board. She said she would talk it over with her husband and let me know. I went back home to wait for word from Alma. After a week I grew impatient, so that Saturday I had Bob take me out there again. She had been wondering when I was arriving. A card had been sent out at once, telling me to come. We stormed back to the house immediately so I could pack what few belongings I had and get out of there. Phil and Carolyn weren't going to let me go. I'm sure Carolyn worried that if I were gone, who would do the chores? Certainly not her. It was a good thing Bob was with me; his presence made me braver so that I could stand up to them and say I *was* going.

My folks were surprised to hear I had left when they got home later that day.

Fred and Alma Seiwart were nice people and very good to me. They had no electricity in the old farmhouse or any of the modern conveniences that I was used to. The bedroom I slept in was cold. But I was grateful to have escaped the clutches of Carolyn. I got up every morning and cooked breakfast for Fred and his nephew before I caught a ride on the school bus. After school I helped make supper and do up the dishes. I also helped with the laundry by bringing in the clothes off the line. Many times during that frigid winter, they were frozen stiff as a board.

I felt badly about abandoning dear Joe, leaving him to fight the battle back home by himself, but at least I could see him everyday at school. He told me he went to friends' houses whenever he had the chance, hoping to be offered

Randolph's first motorized school buses.

some food. I went home on the weekends, to visit, when my parents were there. It upset them that I had left home.

I spent all winter out on the Seiwart farm, while Carolyn was running her new household, charging up a sizable bill at Oh's store that my father would later pay for. John was beginning to get wise to Carolyn's ways. One day when he was home, she came to him with a wedding picture of Phil and her.

"Did you know your sister crumpled this up?"

"Really? Let me see that," John said. It didn't appear to him that the picture was damaged in any way. When he expressed his doubts she said, "Well, I ironed out all the wrinkles." John knew she was lying and began washing his hands at the kitchen sink. He told me he kept washing them over and over so as not to strangle her. Now that John could see her for who she really was, he opened our parents eyes to the truth. It was hard for them to do, but they told Phil he would have to take his wife and baby and leave. They returned to Iowa and I returned home.

I felt guilty, leaving Alma in her condition She had been so kind to me, but I missed being in my own house and wanted to go back to the way life was before Carolyn had come into it. Soon after I had settled back in at home, I learned that Alma lost the baby. I felt just horrible. I eventually found the postcard Alma had sent me, while I was cleaning one day. It was hidden behind some dishes in our China cabinet.

Ten

On Thursday, May 31st, 1934, at the age of twenty years old, I finally graduated from Randolph High School, along with my brother Joe and twelve other seniors. We all stood proudly on the stage that evening, dressed in our finery, and gladly received our diplomas. I remember getting new shoes, a store-bought dress, and a trip to the beauty parlor, all for the big event.

That summer I continued to live at home and kept things running smoothly in the Gilson house-hold. Joe took on a few odd jobs here and there and I cooked and cleaned so things were nice when Mom, Dad and John came home for the weekend.

Although Bob never actually got down on one knee and officially proposed to me, we both knew we would be getting married. We talked about our future together and our love for each other. One evening in August, Bob asked me to meet him in Red Wing. I took the train down and he met me at the depot. From there, we went on to the jewelry store. I was happy to be getting a ring, but I knew Bob wouldn't want to spend too much. I picked out a small, but very nice ring. To my surprise, he wouldn't have it. He picked out a beautiful ¼ carat diamond ring that I'm sure he made payments on for a long time.

Front row L to R: Gertrude Spillman, Myron Witthans, Bernice Wille, Joe Gilson, Verda Reeder, Clair Morrill and Mary Gilson. Back row L to R: Miss Bradford, Marcella Doffing, Marion Ohs, Peter Jamma, Idella Rambo, Andrew Hommertgen, Helen Zwinger, Charles Nelson, Supt. C.O. Nelson.

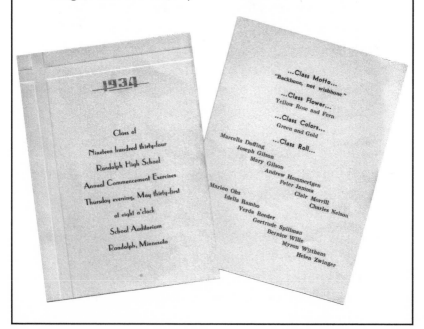

Mary and Bob's wedding
picture.

Mr. and Mrs. Guy Gilson
announce the marriage of their daughter
Mary
to
Mr. Robert E. Ferguson
on Saturday, the third of November
nineteen hundred and thirty-four
Red Wing, Minnesota

My mother wanted me to get married in our family home and I dreamed of walking down the open staircase, looking radiant in the beautiful, frilly gown my mother wore on her wedding day. But we never saw our plans materialize, for Bob had very different ideas. He arranged it all and I knew if I wanted to marry him, I would do things his way.

There was a chill in the air on Saturday, November 3, 1934, but still quite nice for that time of year. At least there was no snow yet. I attended church in Red Wing with my friend, Verda Reeder and her family. We had a nice dinner after the service and then Bob picked me up at the church and took me to the minister's house. Bob looked exceptionally dashing in his fancy suit, shoes, hat and overcoat, all bought brand new for the occasion. He knew how to do it up right and probably saved for months to afford it all.

It was just the minister and his wife. No family or friends were invited. Bob wanted everything to be quiet and low key. It seemed almost secretive to me. We took our vows and then drove to the photographer's studio for our wedding portrait. That was the one arrangement I had made.

For our honeymoon, Bob and I had wanted to go to the World's Fair in Chicago. It had been held over for another year, but we just couldn't scrape enough money together for the trip. Instead we spent a night at the lovely St. Paul Hotel. I remember the room cost $5.00 for the night.

At the time we got married, Bob was earning forty-five cents an hour at the garage in Red Wing. I had no income at all. We certainly couldn't afford a place of our own, so strange as it sounds, Bob lived in Red Wing with his folks and I lived in Randolph with mine. He came to see me every Saturday night and left on Monday morning. This arrangement didn't really suit me. I wanted so badly to have our very own home, but money was tight and Bob thought these arrangements were fine. He wouldn't even think of us both living with his parents. Married life wasn't going quite as I had planned. My daydreams had been brighter than the reality of things, but I had to accept things the way they were, even if it left me sad and lonely at times.

I'll never forget how terribly alone and worried I felt one winter when everyone was gone and a huge snowstorm hit. Bob was in Red Wing; my folks were working; John was called out to plow the tracks from Northfield to Mankato and Joe went with him. It snowed heavily and the bitter wind blew through the uninsulated walls of the big Gilson house. I bundled up and sat on the stairway leading to the basement where the furnace was. The third step from the top was the warmest spot in the house. For four days I was cold, lonely and wondering if the snow would ever end. I was concerned about everyone and their whereabouts. When my brothers finally got home they told me about the snowplow derailing and their being stranded. Mom and Dad made it home, too. I was so glad to see everyone.

Winters got really long back then. I always felt sorry for my dad at that time of year. I used to watch him walk though the deep snow, the flaps of his old flannel cap down around his ears and the collar of his coat up around his neck, trying to keep warm as his aging legs carried him to the depot to get on that train for another week of work. He was getting up there in age and retirement was just around the corner. In July he would celebrate his 65th birthday and the end of his railroad days.

The announcement that came in the spring of '36 was a shock to me. My family was packing up and moving away. Ever since my father had acquired the farm from his cousin Sadie, he had rented it out, but now with his retirement from the railroad in sight, plans were in motion to move to Iowa.

Although Dad still had a few months to go before he could retire, Mom quit working and she, John, and Joe decided to go down first, look things over, and get situated for their new life of farming. Jack Fleming, who was a local trucker and good friend of the family's, helped move the furniture for them. John pulled a trailer behind his car loaded with belongings, too. It was a wet spring in Iowa and the only way to get through some of those back roads was for John and Joe to cut down brush and lay it on the road so the tires didn't sink into the sticky clay.

Their move left me alone in the big, empty house, to listen to the unfamiliar silence and feel the bareness of the walls. Many times I enticed my good friend Idella Rambo to come and sleep with me so I wouldn't be so afraid. Dell, as we all called her, worked as a secretary in the office at school. She says she still remembers the good toasted homemade bread I fed her in the mornings before she went off to work. Thank goodness that kept her coming back because I was scared to death to be all alone in the house at night.

We lived close to the depot, not more than 100 yards away, and there were many bums in those days that hung around the railroad yards. They slept under the water tower at night or stowed away in a boxcar. My mother used to feed them when she was home, before she starting working. One at a time they found their way to our house, hungry and looking for a meal. She never let them come inside the house, but she was always kind to them and didn't turn them away without something to eat. They were told to wait on the side porch while she went in to find some leftovers. She was afraid of the bums, especially if they came in the evening, but her heart was bigger than her fears, and she talked just loud enough to be heard from the porch.

"Well, it could be you someday, poor and hungry. You just never mind," she'd say, as if talking to my father who wasn't really home. She'd carry on a spirited conversation with the walls while she fixed up a plate for those less fortunate. One time, after quite a few had come and gone, she had to tell the last one that he should spread the word: she was out of provisions. No more came up that day.

Now that I was there by myself, I certainly didn't want any bums roaming around outside, looking for a handout of food, or something else.

There was really nothing to do in our small town and the only thing I had to look forward to was Bob and my dad coming home on Saturday nights. They filled the empty rooms with some conversation and brought a little life to the place, but Saturday night all too soon turned into Monday morning and I was left by myself again for another lonely week.

I went down to the farm and stayed for awhile that summer. It was close to unbearable with the heat in Iowa that year. Many days it was 100 degrees or more. The old story and a half farm house certainly wasn't much to speak of—no electricity or indoor plumbing, but there was a welcoming peace. I remember the rusty tin roof on the house. When the rain hit it, it either kept you awake or lulled you to sleep. The house and the farm buildings were built into the hillside of 160 acres. As far as the eye could see, were rolling hills of some of the richest soil in the country. No other houses on the horizon cluttered the view, just sky and earth. As the land sloped down from the house and flattened out into what was called "the bottoms," it met up with Brush Creek, which cut its way through a beautiful woods of red oaks, birch and cottonwoods. Wild phlox grew along its shaded banks, and the old iron bridge crossed over the creek, our route to Rome and Fairfield.

Among the shade trees in the yard, also grew peach, apple, pear and cherry trees that provided wonderful, fresh fruit to eat, some of which my mother canned, or made into pies, preserves and cobblers. She also had raspberry bushes and a strawberry patch. As in the earlier years in Randolph, the family once again had livestock and gardens to supply them with their daily food, but on a much larger scale. There

was space for many more chickens, cows and hogs than they ever had while living in town. A dozen or so head of cattle dotted the clover-filled pasture. Plenty of land was available to raise corn and hay for the animals. In the weathered red barn was room for a team of work horses, and work they did.

John and Joe with Birdy and Topsy.

94

Eventually, John acquired a tractor, but for a few years the fields were tilled, cultivated and harvested by the first kind of "horse power," along with my brother's sweat, muscle, and determination.

Over time, erosion had done its damage, engraving large gullies into the hilly landscape. The renters who had occupied the place for so many years never cared enough to do anything about it. John took it upon himself to terrace the hills so he could farm the land properly. He also took on the huge job of tiling the bottoms, down near the creek. This plot of land was too wet to farm, so John single-handedly placed hundreds of six-inch thick, clay drainage tiles into the heavy mud, using only a narrow shovel and again, hard physical labor. It was a grueling task. He worked very hard on that farm and did so much for my folks. They thought the world of John.

After his birthday in July, Dad officially retired from the Chicago Great Western Railroad. After that many years of hard work and dedication, he was able to draw a pension of $50 a month. He said he never wanted to hear another train whistle blow and moved down to Iowa to join the rest of the family as planned. My problem was I didn't have a plan. I felt as though everyone had abandoned me.

Eleven

A man by the name of Andy Gunderson, a nice, middle-aged bachelor from Zumbrota, came to Randolph and rented out the vacant tavern on Main Street. In the three years since prohibition had been abolished, small bars were springing up in many towns. Andy started up a little business serving 3.2 beer and sandwiches. I heard he needed a waitress so I applied for the job. I figured it would keep me busy so I wouldn't be so lonely. I needed the cash.

It wasn't worthwhile for my parents to have me living in the house all by myself when it could be bringing in some money from renters. So the house was rented out to Mike Maley, a railroad man, and his family. I, in turn, rented a room at Schuler's Rooming House, just around the corner from the bar, for $5 a month. Andy paid me $5 a week as his sole waitress. I had been working there all summer when he decided he wanted to sell the place. Bob and I talked it over and decided we would try our hand at running a tavern. We desperately needed the income. I just never realized how much work I was getting myself into and how tied down I would become.

Bob had always driven old junk cars, but now, for the first time in his life, he had a nice vehicle. It was a fairly new, dark blue Dodge Coupe, and I thought it was beautiful. But it was time to go back to an old model again. Bob made enough money on the car to buy the inventory from Andy and purchase an old 20s Cadillac. It looked like a big, square box with lamps on the inside doorposts that could be lit, although we never did. I frowned on this big elephant, but Bob said, "All bartenders drive big cars!" I never had a chance to drive it, as I was now stuck in the business of cooking for railroad men, serving them beer and trying to be polite in the midst of an unfulfilling marriage and a strong yearning to be back with my family, like in happier times.

Not having a good head for business and no formal training, I made many mistakes. One of them was probably buying the joint in the first place. Another was being too generous. And Bob didn't help matters. He made it a regular practice to treat everyone to a complimentary round on the house. His Scottish tightness disappeared into the bar's haze when it came to drinking. It was more like "buy one, get one free." This practice made a lot of friends but not a lot of money. It was a good thing Bob kept his job at the garage in Red Wing. Bob was still staying with his parents during the week and making the usual weekend trips to Randolph to play husband and bartender. I gave up my room at Shular's and moved in to the living quarters above the bar. The space was more like sleeping quarters than living quarters, for all it amounted to was three or four bedrooms and a bathroom. I suppose we could have made one room into a living room if we'd had a couch and chair or any other furniture to fill it up.

I asked Bob's sister, Peggy, to come and work for me. She moved into one of the rooms upstairs. I waitressed and bartended while Peggy did the cooking, what little there was. People couldn't afford to eat out much. Sometimes on

Sundays Peggy or I would fry up some chickens. Spitzy Miller and his wife lived right behind the tavern. They raised chickens and for $1 I could buy a whole pan, three or four of them, all cut up and dressed. But mostly, we just served hamburgers and hot dogs, and also sold ice cream, peanuts and pop. And of course 3.2 beer on tap, five cents a glass. That's when I first learned to drink beer. The very first time I tasted the stuff I spit it out everywhere. I thought it was awful. I took a small nip at times after that, determined to acquire a taste for the malted brew. Eventually I came to like it. I got to liking it a little too well maybe.

No one in Randolph seemed too creative about giving their business a catchy name. When Andy had the bar, people called it Andy's. When I took it over, they called it Mary's. Simple as that. No fancy sign with hand-painted lettering hung outside the building. Everyone knew who ran it and that's what it was called.

I kept the place open seven days a week, from morning 'til night. There wasn't always a lot of business in the mornings, but if someone came in for breakfast, I rounded up a hot cup of coffee and a donut or some toast. Railroad men were the majority of my clientele. Most of them were good family men from Minneapolis, working for the MN&S Railroad (Minneapolis, Northfield & Southern). They finished their shift in the afternoon, then came over to my place for a few beers, a little cards, and a bite to eat. I had a few extra beds upstairs if they wanted to take a nap for which I charged fifty cents. Some slept from 6:00 in the evening until midnight or so, at which time the hostler, or call boy as he was nicknamed, came to tell them that the train was ready to pull out. Sometimes it was as late as 2:00 in the morning when the hostler came to fetch them. The hostler was the

man who kept the fires going in the engines of the trains and
it was his job also to round up the men for the next shift.

For a while Mr. Cordes and his son Bernard were the
hostlers. Many of the railroad men brought their lunches
from home and kept them in the train near the engine so
they wouldn't freeze. But then the sandwiches began mysteri-
ously disappearing. Some figured it was Cordes and his son
who were stealing the food. In order to prove their theory
and catch the thieves, they laced each sandwich with a small
amount of croton oil and waited. If too much is ingested,
croton oil can kill a person, but in very small doses it is an
extremely powerful, fast acting, laxative. Sure enough, the
sandwiches were missing and so were the hostlers for the
next few days.

Peggy was falling hard for a handsome, young railroad fellow
by the name of Archie Law. His family was from town and
Archie's mother and father were cousins. When Peggy's parents heard about her seeing Archie, they wanted her home.
They did not approve of their daughter getting involved with
this man. According to them, if Peggy and Archie were to get
married and have children, they wouldn't be "right." Kathryn,
Peggy's mother, came in one day very distraught and asked
where Peggy was. I told her she was upstairs, so up the steps
she went, her heels clicking all the way. Kathryn Ferguson had
very tiny feet and always wore little, noisy heels that irritated
me. This day was no different. She was up there ranting and
raving, telling her daughter she would have idiots for children

and when she was all done with her high and mighty speech she clicked back down and out the door. I went up to find Peggy crying. I asked her if she loved Archie and she assured me she did. I told her to forget what her mother said and go ahead and marry him. Her folks didn't want anything to do with me after that, not that they really had much to do with me before. They never seemed to take too kindly to any of their son-in-laws or daughter-in-laws. I think in their eyes, no one was ever good enough for their children.

Bob was supposed to be tending bar and helping out, but he was increasingly distant and absent. He was spending a lot of time with his new buddy, Jack Kipp. Peggy was beginning to get mad at her brother because she wanted some time off to be with Archie. Against her parents wishes, Peggy did

marry Archie in a private ceremony. They rented out a little place in town just a block from the tavern. When Peggy became pregnant she quit working for me. They later moved to Rochester when the railroad transferred Archie there. They

L to R: Archie Law, Joe Gilson, John Gilson, Bill Law, Guy Gilson, and Bob Ferguson.

enjoyed a long, happy married life and raised two bright and handsome sons, Richard and Steve.

Once Peggy quit, and I could see I wasn't going to get much cooperation from Bob, I decided to sell the place. I had run it for about a year but it hadn't been a very lucrative business. Everyone lived on credit in those days—a lot of handwritten IOUs, and many of them went unpaid. Tipping was unheard of. I remember once, and only once, I got a tip. The man who ran the movie theater in Northfield came by one day and asked if I would display his sign showing the movies currently playing. I said sure. He bought a cup of coffee and we chatted. He left me a ten cent tip.

A couple from the Twin Cities bought the place, Grace and Wally Olson, and of course they called it Grace and Wally's. Grace was plenty tight, so they could have made some money, but I think she drank up all the profits.

Jack Kipp and Bob.

Now without a job and no where to live, I just drifted from place to place, staying with friends. I stayed at Marion and Bill Southerland's quite a bit. Marion was a sister to a classmate of mine, Verda Reeder, and both were close friends of mine. Before Marion got married, she taught school in Randolph. I was in the 8th grade, her first year of teaching. Back then they didn't have to go to college for four years to get a teaching degree. A person could acquire a five-year teaching certificate after one year of training. When the five years was up, they had to go on to more schooling in order to continue teaching. I still see her now and then in Cannon Falls where she lives. She plays cards on Fridays like I do. A bunch of us recently helped her celebrate her 95th birthday.

So what a life I was living then: a married woman, lonely, with no home of her own, no job, and a husband, who spent all his time working or with his buddies. I was growing to hate his friend, Jack. I never quite trusted the

Bob inside Klahr's Garage.

man. Jack Kipp was the superintendent of the school. He loved airplanes and chasing women. Bob shared his passion for planes but thank goodness not his other hobby. So while Jack was busy with his carousing, Bob was busy doing whatever Jack wanted him to do, primarily taking care of his precious airplanes.

One thing I was grateful for was Jack letting us live in his trailer house. Bob quit his job in Red Wing and moved out of his parents home. He rented Frank Klar's garage in Randolph again, as he and Ed Brown had done a few years back. This time he ran the auto repair business on his own. We parked Jack's old trailer next to the garage. It was more like living in a boxcar, but at least I knew where I was sleeping each night. We had a carpenter put in some cupboards and I took up housekeeping, trying to make it as cozy as I could.

My maternal instincts were becoming strong at this time. I was twenty-four years old and really wanted to start a family. Bob wasn't much in favor of the idea, but he finally gave in and it wasn't long before I was pregnant. In those days we didn't make a big announcement to everyone. We kept the news quiet until people noticed the weight gain and guessed the reason for it.

I visited a doctor in Red Wing who confirmed my pregnancy. Bob's mother had referred me to him when we were first married. At that time I had been having some pain in my side. He examined me and said I shouldn't have any children and told me my ovaries needed to be removed. I couldn't get out of there fast enough. Everything my mother-in-law had removed had been taken out by him. Thank goodness I never took his advice. I was excited to be with child now.

My brother Joe came back to live in Randolph. He had had enough of farming and country living. Joe was far too restless to be content down there. He rented a room at Schuler's and convinced Lulu Peters to give him a job bartending in the basement of the hotel. What a place to spend any time! It was like a dungeon down there with no windows and a tar-paper floor. To the locals, the place was known as The Basement Bar, but my friend Dell and I nicknamed it "The Blue Room," a fitting name for a place with poor ventilation where everyone smoked.

One time a pilot friend of Bob and Jack's came to town for a visit. I fixed a nice dinner for them all at our house. While the men were occupied with their business of airplane talk, I was to entertain his wife. I had an idea. I suggested we go to the Blue Room for a cocktail. By her expression I could tell she thought I was going to show her Randolph's finest. She changed her expression when we walked down the stairs and into the Blue Room. Dell came with and we both got a kick out of that one.

I was glad to have dear brother Joe back in town and I helped him in his new venture. He was very good to me and did all the heavy work, for I had told him about my condition. He let me sit on a stool at the end of the bar and run the 14 board so I didn't have to be on my feet too much. The 14 board was a shallow, oval-shaped, wooden box, with one end open. It sat on top of the bar and those who wished to gamble a bit could shake the dice into it from a big, leather cup. My memory fails me on just exactly how many turns they had and how it was tallied up, but my job was to oversee it all. It cost a person ten cents to play and instead of winning money, they earned chips, each worth a dollar, which they could trade in for cigarettes, beer and pop.

One night, near closing time, four or five fellows came
down the old steps and each ordered a beer. They weren't
from town; I had never seen them before. One of the guys
sauntered up to the 14 board where I was sitting. He paid his
dime, took his shakes and was a winner, first time out. He
played again and again, each time getting 14. Joe came over
to see for himself what was going on. We knew somehow he
was cheating with an extra dice up his sleeve, but the hand
was quicker than the eye and we couldn't catch him at anything. I don't know how many cartons of cigarettes he ended
up with, but we finally said we had to close up and he and
his buddies would have to go. It wasn't long after they left
that Pauley Gores came in looking upset and angry. He ran
the corner place in Hampton and was wondering if we'd had
some lucky dice players in that evening. They had cleaned
him out earlier.

Lulu eventually had to let Joe go. He was always drunk
behind the bar and that just didn't work out too well for anybody. I loved my little brother Joe with all my heart. Even as
kids we always got along and our friendship followed us into
adulthood. Joe was fun to be with and we had a lot of laughs
together. He was a tall, lean, good looking fellow who loved
to have a good time. He also loved the ladies and booze. He
was seldom without either one. Something he was often
without, though, was money. He got a little loose with his
cash once he had a few drinks under his belt.

Joe started drinking at a young age, and back when he
was 17 or 18, his drinking was a problem. There used to be a
little bar at the end of the block, on the corner right behind
the hotel. Before Otto and Oneva Helgerson owned the
house, the Martins resided in the back and Mrs. Martin ran a
little 3.2 beer joint in the front. One day my mother went

over there and asked her not to serve Joe any more beer. Mrs. Martin refused to serve him after that, but it didn't do any good. Joe went up to Hampton or anywhere else where minors were served. Someone was always willing to take Joe's money, whether he was 21 or not.

Things weren't going very well between Bob and myself. He was out a lot with his group of friends, having a good time and I resented it. I kept long hours at Joe's bar (this was before he got fired) and wasn't home much to cook meals and do the other things a wife was supposed to do.

One time Bob brought some oysters home for me to cook. I had never eaten oysters before and didn't know what to do with them so I found a recipe for scalloped oysters in my cookbook. I fussed all afternoon making a nice meal. I wasn't a very good cook and had a lot of flops, but this dish looked beautiful with the browned bread crumbs on top and all. I was quite proud of myself. When Bob came home and sat down for supper, he looked at the dish and asked, "What's this?"

"It's your oysters!" I tried to sound positive.

"That's not oyster stew," he grunted. He got up and went to the hotel for his supper. I sat at the table and cried. I shed many tears over my failed attempts to please Bob with my cooking. He was used to good food. His mother was a fabulous cook and my mother was, too.

I recall Thanksgiving, long ago in 1938, when I suggested to Bob that we have our Thanksgiving dinner at the Hotel Randolph. That didn't suit him at all. He got mad and left for

Northfield to have dinner. I felt so badly. I went to the hotel by myself, making excuses for Bob's absence. I tried to hide my marital problems, but I'm sure I wasn't fooling anybody.

Time passed and then it was Christmas. Bob went home to be with his parents, not inviting me to join him, so once again we were apart for a holiday. Thank goodness I had Joe and other friends to be with, but this was a sad time for me.

My mother came up for a visit in January and stayed with us in the trailer. It was wonderful to be with her again. I had really been missing her. She and Bob discussed the situation and decided I should go home with her to Iowa until the baby came. I thought it a wonderful idea, to get out of the terrible cold of the trailer and go home to the warmth of my family. I desperately wanted to be with my mother. I wanted to be taken care of. We left on the train bound for Iowa the next day. My mother was so glad to be going home with her daughter and unborn grandchild under her wing that she forgot what day it was. Once we were well on our way, I playfully reminded her of the date. All these years since the tornado she had never stepped out of the house on a Friday the 13th. Until now. She gave a little laugh and said, "I sure hope the train stays on the track!" She finally let her superstition fade as we relaxed to the clickity-clack of the train's wheels. We even splurged and enjoyed a steak dinner in the dining car. That was the first time I had the good fortune to dine on a train and I savored every bite.

Twelve

The winter was cold in Iowa, much as it was in Minnesota. We probably didn't get quite the amount of snow as our northern neighbor, but we weren't far enough south to boast of mild temperatures in January. The cracked walls and crevices of the old farmhouse breathed in the cold air, but the cook stove in the kitchen kept us toasty. Going down to the farm was like stepping back in time. It was more work, yet my parents didn't seem to mind going back to some of the old ways.

Before winter set in, John had hauled in the old, manual washer from its summer residence on the side porch into the kitchen, so Mom could do laundry. Monday was always wash day. She heated up the wash water in a big copper boiler on the cook stove and washed all day. The front porch spanned the whole length of the house on the east side. Instead of trudging through snow out to the clotheslines in the yard, a thin rope was strung from one end of the long porch to the other where we hung up the laundry in those frigid months until it would literally freeze-dry.

Many farm kitchens are big, but this kitchen was humongous. My mother always said she nearly walked herself to death in that big kitchen. That's where I spent most of my time, to stay warm, to be by my mother and to eat. Eating was my new past-time and I fattened up nicely. I wasn't doing much physically like I was used to, and I was eating breakfast, lunch and supper, which I wasn't used to. By my second visit to the doctor, my rapid weight gain made sense. I was told I was having twins! Everyone was excited.

Bob and I kept in touch writing back and forth and made phone calls when the telephone was in service. He came down for a visit after the news of twins. We talked about names and decided if they were boys we would name one, Jim, after his father and the other, John, after my brother. I liked Jean and Jane for girls names but when I even uttered the words "and if they're girls…", he cut me short and grumbled, "If it's girls you can name them yourself," and he walked out of the room. Each night I prayed I would have two boys.

As winter ended, I was getting so big and uncomfortable. Even between my mother's delicious meals I was sneaking into the pantry, snacking on food I had hidden there. The pounds piled on my once skinny frame. Mother sometimes made comments that I should watch how much I ate but my father always reminded her I was eating for two extras. The doctor told me I should walk to get some exercise. I waddled from the house down to the creek and back. It was about three-quarters of a mile one way and it felt good to get some fresh air now that spring was upon us. But soon, even that short stroll became too much, so Mom told me to just walk in the yard around the house. That way she could keep a closer eye on me, too.

A month before I was due, John took me to Fairfield for a doctor's appointment. After the examination, the doctor instructed me to go over to the hospital for an x-ray. He told me he thought he heard three heart beats, which made my own heart nearly stop beating. The prospect of two babies was exciting, but to hear there might be three was quite the opposite. When I got out to the car where John was waiting for me, the shock and despair I was feeling must have shown on my face.

"What's wrong with you?" John asked.

"Why?"

"Well, you look terrible."

"The doctor thinks there are three instead of two," I said with tired hysteria.

His eyes got big. "That's great!"

"Sure, if you're having them." Even as adults, brothers can be stupid. I felt like eating or crying, or both.

I only had to live with the idea of triplets for a few hours. The x-ray showed two babies, much to my relief. I still worried, as did my mother, about giving birth to twins. Both she and my father were concerned about me and my ever growing abdomen. I was huge. Deep down, I really didn't think I would live through it. So I ate all the more, enjoying my last days on earth, sopping up my mother's rich, brown gravy with thick slices of homemade bread, trying to drown my fears the best and most delicious way I knew how. Just to be funny I used to rest the plate on my stomach as I ate.

One day my mother said, "Mary, you have to be prepared, you know. You may not come through this. Have you thought about that?"

"Yes, Mother, I have. The instructions are in my purse." For some time now, I had been carrying a note around which stated my wishes in case I died in childbirth, as many women still did in those days. It was a legitimate fear. The note gave my mother permission to raise the twins in the event of my death. Neither one of us wanted the babies to end up in the hands of Bob's mother. Not that she would even have it. Once, when asked to watch Peggy's kids, she said, "I raised my children—now you can raise yours."

To while away the hours I used to sit and play Chinese checkers with John and my dad on the old wood checkerboard. We also had the big Philco radio in the living room to listen to. Adolph Hitler was going to speak one day and John and Mom wanted to hear what he had to say. They got up at 4:00 in the morning to hear the live broadcast. I didn't have much interest in what was going on half way across the world. I was eight months pregnant and could only think about getting through each day. My concern was surviving childbirth, not what the communists were up to. I left that worry up to the rest of the family.

I stayed in bed that morning but I could hear Mom and John out in the living room. I was drifting back to sleep when I heard John run up the stairs to where my father slept. Since I had come to stay, I slept with my mother in her bed and Dad took one of the rooms in the unheated upstairs. I feared something had happened to Dad the way John tore up there. My dad wasn't doing too well in his old age. I was fully awake now and got out of bed as quick as my pregnant body allowed me to. I went out to the living room to find my mother sitting by the radio with her mouth wide open. She couldn't talk and shooed me away with her hands. She didn't want me to see her and get upset in my condition. By this time John had come back down with my dad right behind him. I asked what was wrong with Mom. John told me she had yawned and her jaw locked up on her. He ran to the phone to call the doctor, only to discover the phone was out of order, as it often was. He jumped in his car and went to the neighbors to call.

In the meantime, Mom used the palms of her hands to massage her face and relax her jaw muscles. Finally, the tightness loosened and she was able to shut her mouth. By the time the doctor got there we were all one big happy family sitting around the kitchen table with Lena gladly fixing us a big breakfast, as usual. She invited the doctor to sit down and eat with us.

Old Doc was certainly relieved. When John had told him to come as soon as he could, "...her jowl is locked!"—the doctor misunderstood. He worried I was in labor, assuming John was referring to me and thought he said, "...her bowels are blocked!"

Coming out to the farm that morning, the doctor saw the springtime condition of our back country roads. He was concerned that when the real time came for me to deliver, he would not be able to get there in time, if at all. In May, we sometimes got a lot of rain and those clay roads became sticky mud that could be nearly impassable, depending on how much rain fell. Doc suggested, as time got closer, I get a room in town. He gave me a name of a woman to contact; a widow living close to the Fairfield Hospital who took people in for a small fee. I visited with her and she seemed nice. Ten days before my due date, I moved in. The accommodations were fine, but she didn't feed me as much as I would have liked. The food was good but not as plentiful as at home. I suppose that was a good thing.

My mother visited me often and slept over a few nights. Bob came down on the weekend of the 20th, which was my due date. When no babies arrived, he headed back to Minnesota in time for work on Monday. The day after he left I started having contractions. Into the hospital I went but it was a false alarm. They kept me there anyway, for they knew the time was near. Just after midnight, on the 25th of May, the real labor began. My mother was called about 5:00 in the morning.

Before she got there I told the nurse I needed to get up and go to the bathroom. I wasn't in there long when all of a sudden there was a huge gush. I pounded on the door for the nurse. "I lost one in the toilet!" The nurse came in and assured me that wasn't the case, my water had just broke. She got me back to bed and then they wheeled me into the delivery room.

Soon I heard the familiar sound of my mother's high heels coming down the hallway's waxed floor. What a welcomed sound. She put on a gown and sat on a chair in a corner of the room. Every time I had a pain I think she had one, too. My back hurt something terrible.

The doctor knew Bob was Scotch and everyone knew the Scotch were tight, so he joked that maybe he should flip a quarter around near my feet which might entice the little ones to come out sooner.

My laboring was long and hard, but by 10:00 that morning I had something to show for it. My first son came into the world, weighing in at 7 pounds 14 ounces, a head of dark hair and squealing for all to hear. I named him James Robert. Twelve minutes later, another son, John Edgar was born. Unlike his twin brother, he was smaller, just 5 pounds 2 ounces, and made no sound. The doctor and nurses worked on him for what seemed like an eternity to get him to breathe. I was so scared he wouldn't make it. My mother was worried too, and said to me, "You'll have to change the name of the first one to John." We both knew how much my brother John had done for me, taking me to all my appointments and how much he did for my folks. If there was to be only one baby he should be named for my brother. Thank

Heaven there was no need to change any names. Little John began to breathe and both babies were healthy and fine. We called Bob right away. My two-week hospital stay cost $150. I was so happy and grateful to be alive with two healthy baby boys, just as I had prayed for.

With the birth of my twins I was forever changed as I'm sure all new mothers are. How does anyone know that motherhood will open up your heart the way it does? So wide open it hurts with vulnerability and pride, with wonder and fear and a sense of overwhelming responsibility. But mostly with love. I suppose the immensity of the openess is to allow all this wonderful new love to flow to and from those little faces.

Faces with innocent bright eyes and skin so soft you can't stop touching it. From that moment on I loved and laughed, rocked and prayed, worried and enjoyed each day more than I ever had before in my life. I welcomed motherhood. I needed those babies.

And, oh how my mother loved her two grandsons. To see them come into this world and know that

Mary, John and Jim.

all three of us were fine was a true blessing to her. My father and John were happy and excited, too.

When the babies were six weeks old Bob came down to take us home to Randolph. Although Bob hadn't originally been too keen on the idea of fatherhood again, he loved his boys. He never showed it, though. That's the way he was raised; there was never open affection in his family, especially between the males. I did see him kiss his mother goodbye on occasion. Sadly, he never hugged his boys or told them he loved them, but in his heart he certainly did and he grew to be very proud of them both.

Bob brought his new family back to Minnesota and into a new house. For $12 a month, we rented a house from the Engler's; therefore, always referred to as the Engler house. It

was a convenient location, just one block from the garage, so Bob could walk to work and home for lunch. At this time Peggy and Archie were still living in Randolph, renting a little house right next door.

While I had been in Iowa, Peggy helped Bob clean, paint the woodwork

⬥———
The Engler house.

and fix up the place so it would be cozy for our return. It was a good sized house with a big kitchen and dining room, but no indoor plumbing. The coolness of the basement was the only refrigeration we had at first. Oh's Store was a block down the street and a daily trip there for perishable items made a refrigerator unnecessary. Eventually, we did get an ice box. Ben Nelson was our iceman. Once, he and Bob had a difference of opinion over something or other and after that Ben starting throwing our ice block in the yard, so I had to walk over to the garage and get Bob to bring the heavy thing into the house before it melted. After Bob and Ben patched things up, Ben went back to putting the ice where it belonged when he delivered it. The ice blocks were cut from Lake Byllesby in the winter and put up on straw in a cement block building where they stayed frozen until needed.

Since the house had electricity, I moved my mother's electric washing machine from the Gilson house into our summer kitchen in the back. When Mom first moved to the farm there was no electricity, when they eventually got it, she still chose to use the old wringer type.

I paid Beatrice McEathron—"Beady" we called her—$1 a week to come every other day and help out. She was one of Evelyn and Florence's younger sister—the McEathrons were a big clan. Each time she came, we washed and line-dried nearly 100 diapers. Although the washing machine was electric, the water still had to be pumped and hauled in from outside, heated on the cook stove, and then dumped into the machine. We didn't have the luxury of disposable diapers or even form-fitted cloth diapers with Velcro tabs and rubber pants like today.

Jim and John kept me busy. If I wasn't washing diapers, I was breastfeeding. I went down to 110 pounds before they were a year old.

It didn't take long for John to catch up to Jim's weight. John was more laid back and quietly sat and played. Jim was more active and on the go constantly. One time, John was contentedly sitting on the floor, playing with the laces of Bob's shoe. Jim was busy getting into one thing after another, when he decided he wanted that same shoe. He crawled over to his brother and tried to take it away, but John wasn't going to give it up and hung on for dear life. Jim crawled into the bedroom and came out with an old slipper of their father's and brought it over to John. John dropped the shoe, grabbed the slipper and Jim got what he was after.

Jim was the first to walk, while John was still happy to sit. Jim would walk to John, take him by the hands, and try to pull him up to teach him to walk. Their antics were always fun. They entertained us as well as each other.

The summer after the boys turned a year old, we went down to the farm for a nice long stay. Peggy always liked my mother, and she offered to go along for a visit and to help with the twins. I couldn't have handled the trip with them by myself. Joe's girlfriend, Viola Ringeisen, missed Joe—he was living with my folks again—and had never been on a train before, so she wanted to go along, too. Viola and Peggy stayed a week and the boys and I stayed all summer.

As usual, it was hot and muggy on the farm. To cool off we filled a big metal washtub with water, and took turns sitting in it in the shaded backyard. Sometimes we went down to the cool, muddy waters of the creek, but we had to be on the lookout for water moccasins. So the boys wouldn't toddle down there on their own, we always told them there were alligators in the creek.

Every morning my mother fired up the cook stove to make breakfast. Unlike the winter months when she kept it going all the time, she let the fire go out until the next meal.

Guy and Lena on the farm.

To cook, bake or do laundry in the summer was always a hot affair. In later years, she bought a kerosene stove she used in the summer and in time, a combination stove.

The summer of 1940 ended and we went back to Randolph. Soon after our return, we moved again into another house. All the while Bob had worked for Jack Kipp, taking care of his airplanes, he did so with no compensation. Jack was a pilot in the Marine Corp Reserves and with the possibility of the United States entering into World War II, he was called to active duty. Bob and Jack struck up a deal. In return for Bob's unpaid services, Jack deeded the small house he and his wife had lived in—they had recently divorced—to Bob. That's how we came to own our very first home. We always referred to it as "the Kipp house."

Mary, Jim and John at the Kipp house.

This time we had all the modern conveniences— indoor plumbing, an electric stove and even a refrigerator. Again, we were close to the garage where Bob worked, just a small field, planted in soybeans, separated our house from the garage. The twins played in the field, picking soybeans and eating them. They didn't have a cold all winter that year—the soybeans kept them healthy.

Bob worked seven days a week, repairing autos and selling gas. I don't recall the price of a gallon of gas back then, since I never had to pay for it. Bob was really mad when Ohs Store put in pumps and starting selling gas, too. Klar's Garage finally had some competition.

Everybody charged in those days. Consequently—just like when we ran the tavern, many debts went unpaid. One night Bob was furious, when a customer came knocking at our door, waking us both up out of a sound sleep. He had filled himself up at the bar and now he was looking to fill up his car so he could weave home. Bob started pumping his gas and asked him how much he wanted.

"As much as you trust me for," the drunk said. Bob shut off the pump right then and there.

Bob had always been interested in engines and enjoyed working with them. He completed the Buick service course at

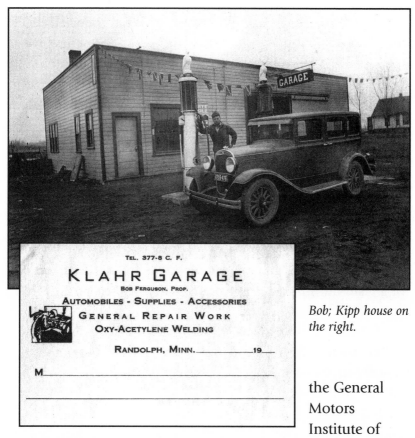

Bob; Kipp house on the right.

the General
Motors
Institute of
Technology in Flint, Michigan back in 1927. Bob was a good
mechanic and saw to it that things were done right. He was
especially interested in airplane engines. He gathered books
about airplanes and studied them every night.

In October of 1940, Bob gave up his business at Klar's
Garage when he was hired by Hinck Flying Service, Inc. at the
Minneapolis airport, as an aircraft and engine mechanic. Not
only did he repair and maintain the aircrafts, but when a
plane went down, he had the painstaking job of inspecting
the engines to determine the cause of the crash. He com-
muted to Minneapolis each day with Clair Morrill, who was a

trainer pilot there. Clair had married my good friend, Dell. They eventually moved up to the cities about the same time that we found a little house to rent, for $35.00 a month, in Richfield—a suburb just south of Minneapolis, close to the airport. We rented out our house in Randolph to Peggy and Archie. I looked forward to the move and a change of scenery. I thought there might be more excitement living in the big city.

Bob still put in seven day work weeks and wasn't around much. The kids rarely saw him. They were in bed at night when Bob got home and not yet up in the morning when he left for work again. I kept busy cooking, cleaning and playing with Jim and John. Once in awhile Bob's folks would come for a visit, but I never saw my family the whole year we lived in Richfield.

On Sunday, December 7th, 1941, while Bob was at work and the twins were playing, the phone rang. It was Dell. She sounded very upset and asked if I had heard the news on the radio. I didn't usually turn on the radio; the kids made so much noise I couldn't listen to it anyway. "Heard what?" I wanted to know. Dell told me the unbelievable news—Pearl Harbor had been bombed. I knew life was about to change for everyone.

The realization that we were actually fighting in World War II weighed heavily on everyone's mind. Talk of the war dominated people's conversations. We listened to news updates on the radio and read the upsetting headlines in the daily paper.

We were already accustomed to getting by with very little, having lived the last decade under the dark cloud of the depression, but to actually have things rationed was different. We got our little books at the beginning of the month and used the coupons for gasoline, sugar, coffee, and meat. When we ran out of those things, we were really out until the next month. It taught us to skimp and save even more than we were used to. Tuna was seven cents a can so we ate lots and lots of tuna, and came up with all kinds of ways to disguise it.

The new Carlton Airport was built in the tiny town of Stanton, just south of Randolph. Bob and Clair were transferred there while we were living in the cities, so they were back to commuting again.

Bob and I talked about moving back and I suggested we find a place in Northfield, but Bob thought we should go back to the Kipp house. We wrote a letter to Peggy and Archie about our plans.

On the day of the move, our friend Jack Fleming loaded up his big truck with all our belongings, and the kids and I rode with him to Randolph. Bob was at work. When the big truck pulled up to the back door of the house, Peggy came out and asked what we were doing.

"We're moving back in."

"Oh no, you're not. You're not moving in here!"

I couldn't believe it. We had given them plenty of notice. I wasn't sure what to do. I walked over to Klar's Garage and used the phone to call Bob at the airport. He came right over, madder than a wet hen, and stormed into the house. Peggy was upset and said she wasn't moving until she got some money for new curtains and other things she needed to buy for a new place. They had a house all lined up and had actu-

Lake Byllesby

1. Gilson House   2. Railroad Depot   3. Hotel Randolph
4. Ferguson House   5. Main Street Tavern

6. *Ohs Store*   7. *Engler House*   8. *Klahr's Garage*   9. *Kipp House*

ally moved all of their stuff, except the kitchen table and chairs. When we came in the back way, into the kitchen, it looked like they were still living there, which is the illusion they wanted to portray.

Bob furiously wrote out a check to Peggy for $30. All of a sudden there was a loud thud outside and we ran out to investigate. Bob had left the Buick in reverse with the keys in the ignition when he had backed up to the porch. John climbed into the driver's seat, started up the car and stepped on the gas. The car hit the porch, leaving a big dent in the bumper.

Poor John got such a terrible licking from his father that day. Bob should have gotten the beating for leaving the keys in the car. Not only was he fuming about his car, but all the anger he felt toward Peggy was taken out on his three-year-old son.

The whole incident over the house built a rift between Peggy and Archie and Bob and me. Peggy and I had always been good friends, but after that we didn't see each other for a long time.

Thirteen

My brother Phil worked at a defense plant in Burlington, Iowa, filling bombs with TNT. Around midnight, a huge explosion occurred. It could have been an accident but some believe it was sabotage. If that was the case, the saboteurs chose the ideal time to injure as many people as possible, for the second shift was coming in and the first shift hadn't

yet left. Some were killed and many severely injured. Phil was blown out of the second floor of the building, into a cinder pile. At the hospital, the doctors had to amputate his foot. Infection soon set in and the leg was removed just

Phil, front left.

below the knee. Strange as it sounds, John buried Phil's leg on the farm, down near the creek. Phil spent a couple of months in the hospital and was fitted for an artificial leg, which he wore the rest of his life. He and Carolyn had three children together: Franklin—who was just a baby when they had lived in Randolph, Raymond and Mary Martha. Carolyn got to running around on him and they divorced sometime after the plant explosion.

It was a sad day for us all, and especially hard on my folks, when John left the farm to serve his country. He was drafted

into the United States Army in 1942. The day Joe accompanied him on the mile and a half walk up to the highway where he was to hail the bus, John told his little brother he had a notion to just keep on walking right over the

John Gilson.

Guy and Lena in Spokane; 1942.

hill and forget about it all. Joe said, "You know you can't, John."

My mom and dad were sick with worry about their beloved John going off to war. Phil would never have to go—he had sacrificed his leg already in the war effort. I'm sure they feared Joe would end up getting drafted, too.

Even though Dad's health was poor, he made the trip with Mom out to Spokane, Washington, where John was stationed in the summer of '42, training as a medic at Baxter General Hospital. The twins and I went with them on the train. We rented a cottage close to the base. I stayed about a week and then took little John home with me. Mom and Dad kept Jim with them and stayed another week.

It was a bittersweet visit. When there is a war being fought and a loved one is involved, you just don't know if you'll ever see him again. The trip was very hard on my dad. He never knew if John returned home safely from the war. That was the last visit he had with his son.

On January 22, 1943, two days after being admitted to the Fairfield Hospital, my father, Guy Gilson, died at the age of 71. Nearly sixty years later the tears still come when I think of losing my father. I loved him.

John was notified and was able to come home on furlough for the funeral. We were all there in Grant Cemetary, in Rome Iowa when they buried him. My mother never shed a tear, that I saw. Her strength during times such as this amazed me.

John left for Spokane, I returned to Randolph, and my mother and Joe went back to the farm to carry on.

By that fall, some major decisions were made. Joe knew it was inevitable that he would be going off to war. He did not want to be in the army, so before they had the chance to draft him, he enlisted in the Navy. Mom made plans for an auction to sell some household items, the farm implements and the livestock; and to move back to Randolph. In November of 1943, John came home on another furlough to help with the sale. I'm sure it was heartbreaking for all of them to see everything go. The farm was rented out to Ernie Hinckle and the Gilsons left their peaceful homestead, sadly going their separate ways. Their hopes were to return someday.

On the 6th of January, 1944, Joe entered active duty and was stationed in Farragut, Idaho. John, now a sergeant, was still stationed in Spokane, and Mother came to live with us in our little house.

Bob and I moved upstairs and gave our bedroom to Mom. It was wonderful to have her around. I always enjoyed

PUBLIC SALE!

As I have rented my farm, I will offer for sale at my farm located 8 miles east of Fairfield on highway 34 to Glendale school and 2 miles north or 2½ miles west of Four Corners, ¼ mile from gravel—

WEDNESDAY, NOV. 10

STARTING AT 10:00 A. M.

12 HEAD OF CATTLE 12

Two Shorthorn cows, 5 years old and milking; 3-year-old roan Shorthorn heifer, milking; two-year-old Shorthorn steer; yearling Shorthorn steer; three Guernsey milk cows, milking; three-year-old pasture bred Guernsey-Shorthorn heifer; month old heifer calf; four months old heifer calf; four months old bull calf.

A Dandy Coming 5-year-old Blue Roan Mare, Weight About 1600 Pounds.

48 HOGS
Five Chester White sows, double treated, with pigs; 42 head shoats, double treated; Hampshire boar.

300 LAYING HENS LEGHORNS & HEAVIES
HAY AND GRAIN

120 bales of timothy hay; 135 bales of oats straw; 225 bushels of oats; about 1000 bushels of new corn, in the crib.

ERNEST HINKLE WILL SELL
Six-year-old bay mare, weight 1100; four-year-old bay horse, weight 1400; three-year-old roan horse, wt. 1150; 17 head of ewes 2 to 5 years old; red yearling steer.

MACHINERY & IMPLEMENTS

1938 Farmall tractor on rubber, if not sold before sale; Little Genius 16-in. gang plow; 7-ft. tandem disc; 21-ft. harrow; 1941 tractor stock cutter; 8-ft. McCormick binder; 1940 McCormick hay loader; 1940 McCormick side rake; 5-ft. David Bradley mower with tongue trucks; good 14-ft. hay rack; two good wagon boxes; high wheel wagon; low wheel wagon; two 4-wheel trailers; two-wheel trailer; dump rake; endgate seeder; Hayes corn planter; walking cultivator; tractor cultivator; scoop board; hand corn sheller; scoops; shovels; pitch forks; mauls; splitting wedges; fanning mill; two prong hay fork; garden cultivator; several circle saws; Galloway No. 10 cream separator; two gas barrels; two oil barrels; several feet native lumber; three good hog troughs; four good slop barrels; ladders; year-old set harness; set old harness; two good 21-in. collars, two pads and many other articles.

HOUSEHOLD GOODS

Good, small size piano; 4 complete bedroom suites; dining room suite; day bed; bedding; electric lamps; brass stand; small table; rockers and chairs; Round Oak range; two heating stoves; oil heater; oil stove oven; brooder stove; lard press; lamps; lanterns; cream cans; sad irons; fruit jars; extra bed springs; curtains; sewing machine; pictures; clock.

MRS. GUY GILSON

Lunch On Grounds
TERMS CASH

Cheney and Van Syoc, Auctioneers
Grant Nelson, Clerk

my mother's wit and wisdom, her good humor and friend-
ship.She was a big help with the boys. It freed up my time
when she kept them entertained and she loved every minute
spent with them. She was a big help in the kitchen, too. Bob
didn't mind his mother-in-law living with us at all. He always
liked my mother and they got along real well.

Thank goodness Mom was still in good health. She
always ate a lot of fresh greens and other vegetables, and got
plenty of exercise through her daily chores. The only ailment
I can ever remember her having is asthma. When we lived in
the Gilson house in Randolph, the meter man gave her a tip
on what to do. He had asthma, also, and took three drops of
kerosene in a teaspoon of sugar. She followed his advice and
claimed this remedy helped.

John got his orders that he was going overseas. Mother
was very upset when we received the news. She traveled by
train out west for a visit in February. Joe was able to meet up
with them, too, and all three were so glad for a chance to see
one another. The following are letters written shortly after the
reunion.

Friday Feb 11, 1944

Dear Joe,

*Mother left yesterday morning. I stayed with her
Wed. night but couldn't see her off on the train yesterday
morning. She rode out to Baxter with me in a taxi and
we said goodbye out here. I know she felt terrible and she
acted so sad it really got me. I can hardly get it off my
mind but she didn't break down while she was with me. I
hope she had a good trip back and feels better when she*

gets back home with Mary. I got a letter from Mary yesterday. Sure hope I can hear from them before we leave here. Don't think we will be leaving until next week sometime but of course we don't know it may be any time. I can't help but think this parting will be for some time. I felt that way when we said goodbye the other night and I just can't stand to say much anymore. I think you felt that way too. I could only send out 3 address cards so 1 to you, 1 to Mary & Mother & 1 to Philip. Thought all the family ought to know before anyone else. You may not get it for some time and maybe never the way things are bawled up around here. But I'll write you every opportunity I have. I hope we can get our mail here, up until we leave. There has been some talk of stopping all mail. But you write anyway and I'll at least have a chance of getting it. It was sure wonderful that I & you & Mother could have that evening together. Think we all feel a lot better about everything. They are still working on the clothing problem here. Issuing checking & exchanging. Looks like they'll never get it straight. I have some to get yet. We'll have practically all new stuff.

How are you getting along with the training now? Hope your chow is better and you don't have so much indigestion. My cold is better but I have been feeling pretty punk. I hope I can get down town tonight. There are a few little things I would like to get yet.

Mary didn't have much to say. Just wished me luck & I think she'll be glad to have Mother with her again. Well Joe hope this finds you O.K.

As ever

John

Randolph, Feb. 15/44

Dear Joe,

Your letter came today, also your insurance receipt and a nice letter from Navy Department. I am enclosing now this $50.00. Will help you on your furlough. I dreaded to bid you boys good bye but was proud of my conduct for I really thought I'd go to pieces and it's a good thing I got started when I did. You know by now that John spent Wed. night with me but the depot wasn't open and we took John to hospital first and I didn't have any trouble at all. Had lower birth. Didn't have any company to speak of but the time didn't seem too long. It was 36 to 38 below coming through Dakotas and Montana and 19 below at St. Paul. The train was 2 hours late so didn't get much sleep and took 820 train to Randolph, the Rochester train. Of course Mary hadn't gotten my card and she didn't expect me. They are all O.K. Bob doesn't know any more than he did. George Ohs has to go for his induction right away. Mary will send you Cordes' address. It's snowing here today. I went out and fed the hens. They look so nice. They get about 70 eggs a day. We will get busy and send you some home-made cookies soon. It's going to be pretty cold to do anything up at the house 'til late in spring so we can make out here. You'll be welcome. Lots of love, Mother. Write often.

Randolph. Feb-15/44.

Dear Joe: your letter came
today also your Insurance
receipt and a nice letter
from Navy Department.
I am mailing now the $5.00
Will keep you on your furlough
I dreaded to bid you Boys
good by but was Proud of
my conduct for I really
thought I'd go to pieces and
it's a good thing I got started
when I did. you know
by now that John spent
Wed night with me but
the depot wasn't open & we
took John to Hospital
first & I didn't have any
trouble alone. had lovely
Birth' didn't have any to
speak of but the trip
seem so long it was
coming through Iowa
and I below at St [...]
there was 2 hou[...]

Dear Joe:
Got your letter this a. m. & so
glad to hear. Mother was so glad to
get to see you. She will be
disappointed if you don't come
here for your furlough. Hope you
decide to as we'd all love
to see you & we've got plenty
of room here for you. I suppose
Bob will be going for induction
next month. Has Ohs gone
Fri. We don't think he'll
pass the physical, but there's
a chance he will. I've always
thought Bob wouldn't, but
right now I think he will.
Let us know just when
you expect your furlough?
Love –
Mary.

Dear Joe,

Got your letter this a.m. and so glad to hear. Mother was so glad to get to see you. She will be disappointed if you don't come here for your furlough. Hope you decide to as we'd all love to see you and we've got plenty of room here for you. I suppose Bob will be going for induction next month. Geo Ohs goes Fri. He don't think he'll pass the physical, but there's a chance he will. I've always thought Bob wouldn't, but right now I think he will. Let us know just when you expect your furlough.

Love,
Mary

Here's a little poem that Joe saved from his Navy days...

Upon the windswept mountain
In a terrible spot,
Battling the terrible snowstorm
In a spot that God forgot,
Up near the top of the mountain
Up where a man gets blue,
Fifty miles from the nearest town
And fifteen hundred from you.
At night when the wind is howling,
It's more than a man can stand.
No, we're not convicts,
We're defenders of our land.
We're sailors in the service,
We earn our meager pay,
Saving Wall Street's millions
For a buck and a half a day.
Not many know we're living,

And not many give a damn
Back home, we're soon forgotten
We're lent to Uncle Sam
And when the war is over
And we're returning to our gals
We'll only find them married,
To some of our God damned 4F pals.

Joe Gilson.

When the troop train came through town, the service men hung out the windows, waving the letters they wanted mailed off to their loved ones. I used to help out by taking their letters to the post office for them. Postage had gone up to three cents.

Many fine young men from Randolph were going off to war. Bob wanted to be one of them. I was terribly upset when he enlisted in the U.S. Marine Corp as a mechanic. I was so worried about my brothers and what was to become of them all, and now my husband was leaving me with two small children. It was a tearful farewell on my part, the morning Bob packed up to go. There were no tears from Bob, however. Not even a hug for me or the boys, just a simple "goodbye."

That evening, the phone rang. It was Bob. "You'll have to come to Hampton and get me. I'm not going," was all he said. I bundled up the twins on that cold March evening and chipped the ice off in front of the garage door so I could get it open.

The Marines had rejected him because of the bad curvature of his spine. His back had been that way ever since I knew him, but Bob had never talked about it. I don't know if he was born with the deformity or if it was scoliosis that caused it, but it prevented him from going off to war. I was relieved.

The renters at the Gilson house moved out, so Mom decided she would like to fix it up and move back in. We were all getting a little crowded at our place and she thought it would be a good idea if we moved in with her.

Tony Kruze, a good friend and great carpenter, was hired for the remodeling job. He ripped up the old flooring and replaced it with beautiful hardwood floors. I worked right along side Tony, helping him in any way I could. We worked there all summer long, putting in new cupboards and fixing it up nicely. It took all Mom's money but she felt it was worth it.

Bob didn't want us to move into the house with my mother. The twins would be starting school soon and he didn't want them to have to cross the railroad tracks to get there. Our house was so nice and close, half a block from the school. I told him the boys and I were going, whether he came or not, and he knew I meant it. He decided to come along.

His father had retired from the railroad and he and Kathryn were still living in Red Wing. Bob talked them into moving back to Randolph and living in our little house. They did and eventually bought the place from us for $4,000.

Mom bought a cow and some chickens, and loved being back in her house. I loved being there, too, and so did the twins. It was a great place for two five-year-olds.

As the war continued, my mother's once good health began to decline. She worried so about her boys. Each day I tried to get the newspaper before she got to it. If the headlines were too depressing, talking about how many soldiers had been killed, I hid it. She was a nervous wreck. There were times when we didn't hear from John or Joe for a month or more.

Mom had always been a good-sized woman, 150 pounds or better, but the stress of not knowing if she'd ever see her sons alive again caused her to drop to 125 pounds. She didn't like getting thinner, so she wore a belt around her waist under her dress and layered a towel over the belt. This way she looked nice and plump through the middle.

Lena, Jim and John at the Gilson house.

Bob took on a new job at an arms plant in Rosemount. Soon, a file clerk position became available there; I applied for it and got the job. Mom took care of the twins while Bob and I were at work, but they became too much for her. We made an arrangement with the Nelsons. Ben, who had been our ice-man at the Engler house, worked at the same plant, so in exchange for giving him a ride to work, his wife Edna babysat the boys.

Mom continued to go downhill, so after just a few months of working, I quit to be home with her.

In August of '45, while John was somewhere in Europe and Joe was on a ship off the coast of Japan, the United States dropped the atomic bomb on Hiroshima and a few days later did the same thing at Nagasaki. Joe watched from out at sea and later told us, "The whole world looked like it was on fire when we dropped that bomb."

Within a week the war was over and those who had survived slowly began to return home to their families. Thank God, John and Joe were among them, although it wasn't until January of '46 that we welcomed John home. Joe returned in March. It was wonderful and such a relief the war was over, but my heart went out to the many families that never saw their loved ones again.

Army of the United States

Honorable Discharge

This is to certify that

JOHN L GILSON   37 193 125   TECHNICIAN FOURTH GRADE

82ND GENERAL HOSPITAL

Army of the United States

is hereby Honorably Discharged from the military service of the United States of America.

This certificate is awarded as a testimonial of Honest and Faithful Service to this country.

Given at   SEPARATION CENTER
CAMP MC COY WISCONSIN

Date   13 JANUARY 1946

State of Iowa
Jefferson County. } ss.   DEC 19 1946
At 8:30 o'clock A. M., and Recorded
in Book 5 on page 232
of Jefferson County Records.

Virginia R. Oliver
Recorder

Thomas B Hammond

THOMAS B HAMMOND
MAJOR, AGD

ENLISTED RECORD AND REPORT OF SEPARATION
HONORABLE DISCHARGE

1. LAST NAME - FIRST NAME - MIDDLE INITIAL	2. ARMY SERIAL NO.	3. GRADE	4. ARM OR SERVICE	5. COMPONENT
GILSON JOHN L	37 193 125	TEC 4	MD	AUS

6. ORGANIZATION	7. DATE OF SEPARATION	8. PLACE OF SEPARATION
82ND GEN HOSP	13 JAN 46	SEPARATION CENTER CAMP MC COY WIS

9. PERMANENT ADDRESS FOR MAILING PURPOSES	10. DATE OF BIRTH	11. PLACE OF BIRTH
RANDOLPH MINN	18 JUL 11	CLARION IOWA

12. ADDRESS FROM WHICH EMPLOYMENT WILL BE SOUGHT	13. COLOR EYES	14. COLOR HAIR	15. HEIGHT	16. WEIGHT	17. NO. DEPEND.
SEE 9	GREY	BROWN	5-8	147 LBS.	1

18. RACE	19. MARITAL STATUS	20. U.S. CITIZEN	21. CIVILIAN OCCUPATION AND NO.
WHITE X	SINGLE X	YES X	LINEMAN POWER 5-53.420

MILITARY HISTORY

22. DATE OF INDUCTION	23. DATE OF ENLISTMENT	24. DATE OF ENTRY INTO ACTIVE SERVICE	25. PLACE OF ENTRY INTO SERVICE
28 APR 42	28 APR 42		FT DES MOINES IOWA

SELECTIVE SERVICE DATA ► 26. REGISTERED YES X | 27. LOCAL S.S. BOARD NO. #1 | 28. COUNTY AND STATE JEFFERSON CO IOWA | 29. HOME ADDRESS AT TIME OF ENTRY INTO SERVICE SEE 9

30. MILITARY OCCUPATIONAL SPECIALTY AND NO.	31. MILITARY QUALIFICATION AND DATE
X-RAY TECH 264	NONE

32. BATTLES AND CAMPAIGNS — NONE

For convenience, a copy of serial No. 53 10730 has been issued by the Veterans Administration to be used for the future request of any guaranty or insurance benefit under title III of the Servicemen's Readjustment Act of 1944, as amended, that may be available to the person to whom this separation paper was issued.

33. DECORATIONS AND CITATIONS — GOOD CONDUCT MEDAL

34. WOUNDS RECEIVED IN ACTION — NONE

35. LATEST IMMUNIZATION DATES				36. SERVICE OUTSIDE CONTINENTAL U.S. AND RETURN		
SMALLPOX	TYPHOID	TETANUS	OTHER (specify)	DATE OF DEPARTURE	DESTINATION	DATE OF ARRIVAL
JAN 44	SEP 45	MAY 44	TYP FEB 44	28 FEB 44	ETO	12 MAR 44
				20 DEC 45	USA	7 JAN 46

37. TOTAL LENGTH OF SERVICE					38. HIGHEST GRADE HELD
CONTINENTAL SERVICE		FOREIGN SERVICE			
YEARS	MONTHS	DAYS	YEARS	MONTHS	DAYS
1	10	5	1	10	10	SGT

39. PRIOR SERVICE — NONE

40. REASON AND AUTHORITY FOR SEPARATION — CONVENIENCE OF THE GOVT RR1-1 (DEMOBILIZATION) AR 615-365 15 DEC 44

41. SERVICE SCHOOLS ATTENDED — NONE

42. EDUCATION (Years)		
Grammar	High School	College
8	4	0

PAY DATA

43. LONGEVITY FOR PAY PURPOSES	44. MUSTERING OUT PAY			45. SOLDIER DEPOSITS	46. TRAVEL PAY	47. TOTAL AMOUNT, NAME OF DISBURSING OFFICER
YEARS 3 MONTHS 8 DAYS 6	TOTAL $300	THIS PAYMENT $100		NONE	$16.45	107.98 M L OLDENBURG MAJ FD

INSURANCE NOTICE

IMPORTANT: IF PREMIUM IS NOT PAID WHEN DUE OR WITHIN THIRTY-ONE DAYS THEREAFTER, INSURANCE WILL LAPSE. MAKE CHECKS OR MONEY ORDERS PAYABLE TO THE TREASURER OF THE U.S. AND FORWARD TO COLLECTIONS SUBDIVISION, VETERANS ADMINISTRATION, WASHINGTON 25, D.C.

48. KIND OF INSURANCE				49. HOW PAID		50. Effective Date of Allotment Discontinuance	51. Date of Next Premium Due (One month after 50)	52. PREMIUM DUE EACH MONTH	53. INTENTION OF VETERAN TO		
Nat. Serv.	U.S. Govt.	None		Allotment	Direct to V.A.				Continue	Continue Only	Discontinue
X				X	X	31 JAN 46	28 FEB 46	7.20	X		

54. (blank)

55. REMARKS (This space for completion of above items or entry of other items specified in W.D. Directives)
EUROPEAN-AFRICAN-MIDDLE EASTERN THEATER SERVICE MEDAL
AMERICAN THEATER SERVICE MEDAL
THREE (3) OVERSEAS SERVICE BARS
LAPEL BUTTON ISSUED
ASR SCORE (2 SEP 45) 60

RIGHT THUMB PRINT

56. SIGNATURE OF PERSON BEING SEPARATED	57. PERSONNEL OFFICER (Type name, grade and organization - signature)
John L. Gilson	Carl Butler — CARL L BUTLER 2D LT AC ASSISTANT ADJUTANT

WD AGO FORM 53.55 1 November 1944. This form supersedes all previous editions of WD AGO Forms 53 and 55 for enlisted persons entitled to an Honorable Discharge, which will not be used after receipt of this revision.

The tavern on Main Street that I had run years earlier had closed during the war, like so many businesses, and now sat empty. I brought up an idea to my friend Viola Kruze, Tony's daughter, who was married to Carl Johansson. Her husband had fought in the war and was due back soon, along with my brothers and many others from Randolph. I said to Viola, "Here these boys will all be coming home soon and the town will be hopping. We should get this place running again." She was all for it.

Jim and John were in the first grade and in school all day. My mother could watch them in the evenings, for her health had greatly improved now that the war had ended. Her worries were over, knowing her boys would soon be with her.

So Viola and I got the tavern up and running again. Before Carl came home, I told Viola I would step out if she and Carl wanted to run the place together. There wasn't enough income to support two families. But when Carl returned home, that was the end of Viola working with me. He didn't want either one of them to have anything to do with the tavern.

I ran the place by myself for awhile longer, but there really wasn't as much business as I had anticipated.

Fourteen

The future was looking brighter and people were celebrating better times to come. Joe and I enjoyed going out for a few drinks occasionally. It was still just 3.2 beer in Randolph, but if we went to Hampton we could get hard liquor. Bob never much cared for the idea of me going out with my brother, but he didn't know most of the time. He was out with his buddies doing his own share of drinking.

Mother used to get so mad at Joe and me. One night we had been out having fun, and when we came home I went straight to bed. After I'd been asleep awhile, Jim and John came into my room and said, "Mom, wake up. Something smells funny." I dragged myself out of bed and down to the kitchen.

Joe had gotten hungry and was warming up the leftover pot roast. He had also made himself a plateful of scrambled eggs which he was seated in front of at the table, his face laying directly in them. The charred roast filled the kitchen with smoke. Mother was so angry at us, and the black-ened wall above the stove didn't soften her mood.

For a short time, we lived in Rosemount where Bob had
hooked up again with Jack Kipp in another venture. Jack, Bob,
and Helmer Johnson formed a business called the Southport
Aero Service. As a newspaper article described it...'The airport
will specialize in aircraft sales, maintenance and repair, hangar
rental, flight and ground instruction, and charter service.'

I didn't want to move and after a month I longed to go
back to Randolph. Being so close to all the activity of the airplanes was not a safe place for the boys. Jim was nearly killed
one day as he ran toward a plane just as it was starting up. I
screamed and caught him in time. Who knows what the force
of that big propeller would have done to him.

That was the last straw for me. Bob and I got in a huge
fight. I packed up my things, took the boys, and left. Few ever
knew this, but I filed for divorce. When Bob was served the
papers, I can only imagine the advice from his friend Jack.
Wives were easy come, easy go to him—he was on his third
marriage at the time—but Bob was a better man than that. He

Bob.

quit the whole operation at the airport, came back to the boys and me, and never had much to do with Jack Kipp after that.

Although Bob got along well with my mother and brothers, being back among all the Gilsons didn't really suit him. I didn't mind a bit, but looking back, I can see his point. When John and Joe came home from the war and Phil came to stay with us after his divorce, Bob referred to it as an invasion.

The full house soon quieted down. When Ernie Hinckle's lease on the farm was up, Mom and all my brothers happily returned to the Iowa countryside. This time they farmed some of the land and rented out the rest. John also worked for the REA (Rural Electric Association), and Phil got a road maintenance job with the county, grading the roads.

Mom did what she knew and loved: cooking, canning, gardening and raising chickens. Although she rarely followed recipes, I recently found this one written in her handwriting on a little piece of paper.

Lettuce Salad Dressing

Take the yolk of three hard boiled eggs, add salt and mustard to taste. Mash up fine. Make a paste by adding a dessert spoon of olive oil or melted butter. Use butter when it is difficult to get fresh oil. Mix thoroughly. Then dilute by adding gradually a teacup of vinegar and pour over the lettuce.

She picked dandelions from the yard, using the greens in salads and making her own wine from the dandelion blos-

soms and grapes she grew herself. One day, while down in
the cellar getting some canned goods, she thought she might
sample the jugs of wine to see if they had aged long
enough. When the boys came in for lunch, they didn't smell
the usual aroma of good cooking and no sign of Mom anywhere. They noticed that the cellar door was open and
hollered down. Mom answered from her perch on the bottom step, "I'm down here." Her taste test was a bit much for
her and she felt too unsteady to make it up the rickety stairs
to the kitchen. My brothers had a good chuckle over it all as
they helped her back up. She never let that happen again.

As had happened many times before, Joe's restless spirit
yearned for something more than farm life could provide. In
the Navy he had received some electrical training. Joe was interested in that kind of work, so he moved to St. Paul where he
took further instruction in hopes of becoming an electrician.

Joe's goal was realized in May of 1948 when he passed
his exam, certifying him as a licensed Journeyman electrician.
He made good money at his trade but he drank it all up. He
often visited the boys and me on the weekends and we
looked forward to seeing him, but sometimes it was a two-
day binge for him. Jim remembers finding his uncle Joe on
the couch one afternoon, covered with dried blood, passed
out cold and reeking of alcohol. We later found out that Joe
had borrowed Elaine Andrews' '36 Ford and gone to
Hampton to drink. On his way back, he lost control of the
car on a curve and rolled it.

At other times, Joe would be on good behavior and announce that he had quit drinking. But it was always short lived. With his reckless good looks and care-free attitude, Joe was a ladies man. He had lots of girlfriends, but none of them lasted long. Although Joe was a happy drunk and never got mean or ugly, his alcohol abuse eventually drove the women away.

The following is a letter Joe received from our brother John in the summer of '47.

June 11, 1947

Hi Joe,

Guess this will about bowl you over, getting a letter from me. I've said I was going to write for months but perhaps you know how easily letters are put off. Of course we hear from Mary quite often and she lets us know how you are getting along. Mary and kids should be here next week at this time. Guess I'll meet them at Albia. We have been having the wettest weather I've ever seen here and suppose you have heard all about the floods. Ottumwa was the worst in history. We are quite comfortable here on the farm again. But haven't done anything towards fixing things up as we want them. Don't have very much time it seems. I have to leave my car on the gravel and walk. It is raining again tonight. The farming has been terrible. We rented to the Nelson boys, Cecil and Willard. They have the west bottom and just east of barn in corn and its wet and weedy. They have the east bottom about ready and the middle bottom to plow for beans yet. We got an old county grader and I laid off 3 days and we made a new drainage ditch down thru the bottom. It is working good so far. I have a cow to milk

and a sow to feed. Bought the cow and calf for $200 in
April and the sow in May, $82.50. Outrages, isn't it?
But she's a wonderful cow. 5 gallons per day. And the
sow will have pigs in a week or two now. The calf is
worth $60 they tell me but guess we will keep it for beef.
We eat lots of meat and have a locker at Lockridge. The
hills are all seeded down and I'm fighting weeds and
sour dock every spare minute. We have a pretty nice garden and 50 baby chicks and 4 old hens. Guess that is all
on the farming. When are you paying us a visit Joe?

Did you pass your exam o.k. and get in the union?
Almost wish I had stayed in Minnesota now. We are having a good deal of labor trouble at R.E.A. I'm getting
$.95 now. We all joined the Union a few weeks ago.
What a hotbed. The board of directors met last night. We
got the ultimatum this morning. They fired Slim and I
said you can make out my time along with Slim's but the
union man came up and told us to all go back to work
but Slim, and guess his time will go on just the same. We
have a crew of 19 men now so guess they will come to
terms. Russell is fighting us tooth and nail but says he
has our best interests at heart. He's a skunk Joe, and is
showing his color now. He can lie faster than a guy can
think. We have a "scab" in the bunch, Herbie Baker's
son-in-law. I think he was put in as a stool pigeon. I'll be
glad when it's all settled and I may quit. I've been fed up
with the job for a long time. But the union may
straighten things out. I do hope you get in the union and
can keep your job o.k. I think when the scare is over we
will have some hard times. But as long as there is war in
the air guess things will stay about as they are. Bob H.
went in the Naval reserve last week. He says if anything
comes up he can go back in at his old rate. Bob is doing

*o.k. I trade there, that is stop almost every night for gro-
ceries. Saw Bud B. and his mother last week. Mr.
Baldosier died not long ago. Bud looks fine and seems
the same. I promised to go down fishing sometime. The
"Skunk" [River] is out over everything but going down
gradually. Five straight years the bottom farmers have lost
out. Don't see how they stand it. Well Joe, I'll try and
write more often and wish you would too. Haven't heard
from Phil lately. We were supposed to have had his kids
for a week but Carolyn got a "bug" at the last minute
and wouldn't let them come. We never have had them.
Well, such is life I guess. The little girl always acts like
she would just love to be with us but Carry has the club
over our heads now. Let me hear!*

John

Back when John was trying to get the farm going again,
he had to visit his banker on occasion. One time he went in
to borrow $500 to buy some more cattle. The banker said
he'd make a deal with him. If John had $500, the bank
would match it and loan him another $500. John was furi-
ous. "If I *had* $500, I wouldn't be in this damn bank!" and he
stormed out.

John and some of the buddies he worked with broke
away from R.E.A. and formed their own business, running
high line (big transmission lines) across Nebraska. He came
home on the weekends now and then. Phil was there to keep
up the farm.

John and his partners all had money stuck into the business, for start up costs and buying the big, heavy equipment
they needed. They worked hard but their bookkeeper was
crooked and pocketed most of the money. Eventually, the
business folded and John settled down to farming once again.

June 11, 1947

Hi Joe,

Guess this will about bowl you over, getting a letter from me. I've said I was going to write for months but perhaps you know how easily letters are put off. Of course we hear from Mary quite often and she lets us know how you are getting along. Mary should be here ti...

John Gilson
Lockridge, Iowa

Joseph Gilson
630 Ashland Ave. apt. 18
St. Paul,
Minnesota

...me it seems.
...leave my car on the gravel & walk. It is raining again tonight. The farming has been terrible. We rented to the Nelson boys. Cecil and Willard. They have the west bottom and just east of barn in corn and wet & weedy.

Fifteen

Back in 1946 Bob bought a parcel of land east of town. Now, with the anticipation of a new highway going in, which was to run north and south, along the property line, Bob knew he'd made a wise purchase. It was a prime location for a business. We discussed building a nice tavern there.

Bob's dad, "Grandpa" as we always referred to him after the twins were born, also had some ideas for that spot. He talked of putting up a gas station there, and his son Jimmy could run it.

I thought it sounded like a good opportunity to make some money. Although it was never my life's ambition to own a restaurant and bar, it was about all I knew how to do. My mother fed people all her life—her family and friends, boarders, railroad men, and bums. I guess my life had followed a similar path of serving food to people, but—unlike my mother—I served them drinks, too. It looked like I was going to continue doing so.

An adjacent lot was purchased, plans were drawn up, money was borrowed, and our ideas became a reality. In 1949, the Lakeview Inn was built. Tony Kruze was hired as the carpenter and Harold Swanson did the tiling and woodwork. One day, Harold had just finished laying the kitchen floor when I walked in and nearly fainted.

LAKEVIEW INN
"A Place of Refreshment"
RANDOLPH, MINNESOTA

Grandpa, thinking he was the boss, had ordered the ugliest black and brown linoleum floor tiles ever made. I raised such a ruckus and insisted that all tiling stop. When the new lighter-toned squares that I chose arrived, tiling resumed. I lived with that ugly kitchen floor all those years as a reminder of what poor decorating taste my father-in-law had, and thankful the public didn't have to endure it.

In my eagerness to get things done, I gladly helped Tony and Harold, varnishing and tiling. While Harold laid the dining room tiles, I worked on the area behind the bar. If I messed up, no one would see my mistakes back there. Bob came home from work one evening, while Harold was finishing up with the floor, and commented, "Gee, you got a lot done today!"

"Well, Mary helped, too. She did all the tiling behind the bar."

Bob was surprised. "She did?" He looked things over closely, trying to see my mistakes, but he found none.

We had small, but nice living quarters in the back consisting of a front room with space for a dining table, one bedroom, a bathroom, and a partially finished half story upstairs where the boys slept. It was wonderful to have a brand new place to live.

For the first several years I had a small business serving 3.2 beer and hamburgers. I enjoyed socializing with my customers and made many new friends. I didn't have time to go out drinking and dining with people. I didn't need to, they came to me. I also didn't have the time or the need to spend money on clothes for myself. My daily attire was a uniform and an apron.

Bob was good with the maintenance of the place, keeping the furnace and all the things I knew nothing about, running

Bob (kneeling) at Lake Byllesby.

well. He was doing some commercial fishing in the winters down at Lake Byllesby. The state's Fish and Game Department paid him two cents a pound to take the rough fish out (carp, buffalo fish, bullheads, sheep heads, and suckers) using huge nets. All the carp went to local farmers for pig feed. Bob hauled the buffalo fish to holding tanks at Sorenson's Fish Market in Bay City, Wisconsin. There they boxed and iced the fish and shipped them out East. There was a big market for them in the Jewish communities of New York.

Although we had a good banker who would loan us money when we needed it and let us pay when we could, it meant we were deep in debt. With things slow in the restaurant, and the fishing just seasonal, Bob signed up with North Atlantic Constructors who were advertising the need for men to help build an airport in Greenland. The pay was excellent, as it would have to be to get people to work in those frigid conditions. This job really kept us afloat. He made eight trips to Greenland, over the course of eight years, leaving every spring and staying about five months each time.

I never worried about myself when he was away, but I worried about the boys. I kept close tabs on them. If they were to get into trouble, Bob would surely blame me. Thankfully, they were good kids and stayed out of any major mischief. They had chores to do before and after school, such as filling the pop and beer coolers, and sweeping the floor.

Some may have thought I wasn't a good parent—raising my children in a bar, but I took good care of them. They were clean, nicely dressed and well fed. And I loved them.

By the winter of '51, business was slim. There were days when no one came in at all. A lot of people seemed to be out of work, including Bob and Joe. Bob had been hired for the Greenland project, but wasn't scheduled to leave until spring. Joe was laid off, so he gave up his apartment and moved in with us. When he had lived and worked in St. Paul, he came down on weekends and bartended for me once in awhile. But now, in exchange for his room and board, I had Joe for a full-time bartender. The problem was I had few at the bar for him to tend.

Bob liked Joe, but he didn't like his drinking. Although Bob drank himself, he never got drunk. He knew when to quit and always remained a gentleman. Joe tried to stay on Bob's good side, but living in a bar with his brother-in-law wasn't the best place for Joe.

Mom and Phil came up for a visit that winter, so I had plenty of time to spend with them. Since things were so slow, I thought it a good time for the twins and me to go back with

Jim and John.

Mom and Phil for a retreat to the farm. Bob and Joe could handle what few customers there were. After all, I had a free ride, so we all packed up for the eight-hour drive to Iowa in Phil's '38 Pontiac.

Jim and John were in the sixth grade and walked two miles on snow-drifted roads to Harmony #9 each school day. They helped with chores and spent time with their grandma and uncles. A half dozen cows, milked by hand, kept them busy.

Every morning they took turns emptying the chamber pot, or "slop jar" as we called it. Some mornings it was so cold in that back bedroom there was a thin layer of ice on the top of the pot's contents. The heavy quilts were piled nearly a foot deep on the beds. As soon as the boys got out of bed, they grabbed their clothes and ran to the kitchen to dress. It was always warm there, with the cook stove fired up.

Being on the farm was like a vacation for me. I enjoyed helping Mom with the housework. Bob and I kept in touch writing letters back and forth.

Minnesota was getting its share of a cold winter also. A snow storm brewed one Thursday night when Joe and his buddy, Bob Anderson, were out on the town.

The two were on their way to Red Wing, on Highway 19, when they stopped at a little store in Vasa to get some mix. While Bob was in buying what they needed, something compelled Joe to slide over to the driver's seat and take off. Maybe it was meant to be a joke. Maybe Joe planned to stay gone just long enough to make his friend wonder what was up. Maybe Joe thought he would show up after a bit and they could have a good drunken laugh about the whole thing.

But Joe didn't come back and Bob was in no laughing mood when he called his friend, Doug Anderson, to come and pick him up. The two men searched all night in the blowing snow, but couldn't find Joe.

The next morning, with the blizzard over, a man walked down to the end of his driveway to get his mail and noticed the mangled car upside down in the ditch, half buried in snow. He called the authorities and the mystery of what happened to Joe was over. So was his life at 34 years of age.

My husband called me with the horrible news. Although the circumstances of Joe's death didn't surprise me, I was devastated just the same. Not only had I lost a loving brother, I had lost my life-long friend.

John and I drove up to bring our little brother back home. The railroad required a family member to accompany the body, so I rode the train back with Joe's remains, and John drove the long way back by himself.

Joe's funeral was the only time I ever saw my mother cry. It was the first time I ever touched a corpse. I remember it as cold and hard; I remember the scar on his face.

Our first night back in Randolph, while Jim was trying to fall asleep, he felt something, someone, touching his back. He believes it was Joe's spirit. Jim was lying in the bed that Joe always slept in when he stayed with us.

Sixteen

Shortly before Bob was to go to Greenland for the first time, I discovered I was pregnant. I felt like the world was crashing in on me. My husband was about to leave the country for a half a year, I had two teenage boys to raise, a business to run, I was still grieving the loss of my brother, and now I was going to have a baby.

Bob and I both knew he would still have to go to Greenland, he had signed a contract and wouldn't have the opportunity to go again if he broke it. Plus, we just couldn't pass up the money. The day he left, he gave me a hug, shook Jim and John's hands and told them to be good, and then he was gone. I knew I would have to make the best of things, but I wasn't too sure how I was going to go about it.

Bob had been gone a few months when I began to miscarry. It may have been the stress and worry that caused it, I don't know. The doctor put me in the hospital where I stayed for a few days. I suppose it was for the best, but it still saddened me to lose a child.

I had Harry Felton to take care of things at the restaurant during my recovery. Harry was a bachelor, poor and alone, who had lived in an old boxcar by the East/West tracks, the Doodle Bug track. That winter, when I had been in Iowa, someone came to Bob and told him how old Harry was freezing to death at his place and something had to be done. Bob took him in. He hung a curtain in a corner of our basement to partition off a room for him. Harry was there when the twins and I came home from the farm.

I didn't mind. Harry was a good man—harmless, clean and never swore. In exchange for his room and board, he swept the floor, and wiped down the tables and booths. It was nice to have someone lighten the load for me. This arrangement went on for three or four years.

Not only did he get a bed and meals, but I kept him supplied with snuff. Along with his chew, Harry liked his beer. He had a perfect set up in the basement, right next to the walk-in cooler. Every once in awhile I'd hear the heavy door of the cooler open and shut. Then it got to the point that he was in there half the time. When Harry got to drinking, he got silly—laughing and talking to himself. As the years went on, he drank more and worked less.

One day I went downstairs just as he was going into his room. Before he closed the curtain, I spied a case of beer on the floor. "Oh, I see you're taking it by the case now." Harry told me to shut up and go upstairs.

"That will be enough now," I said. I knew something had to be done. I called his sister-in-law, who was married to his brother Bill, and asked if she wanted Harry.

"Hell no! I don't want him. I've had enough of him in my time."

When Bob returned from Greenland that year, I told him about the problems with our houseguest. "You brought him here, you get rid of him," I said.

Bob had a talk with him. "Mary tells me you've been drunk all summer. You'll have to hit the road, Harry." We called his sister Ester and she agreed to take him in. She was married to a Klahr and they lived on a farm. Harry gathered eggs and did other small chores for them. No drinking was allowed at their place and it was too far to walk to town to get drunk. We all thought that was a good place for him. All but Harry. He eventually got back to town and back to drinking. He and a few other homeless men from Randolph finally ended up in the Vet's Home in Hastings.

I had to be careful, a woman alone, with strangers coming in off the highway. One dark, blustery night, no one else was in the place except a guy I had never seen before. I was back in the kitchen, cleaning up, while he ate a late supper with his beer. Before I knew it, he was in the kitchen with me. A butcher knife was laying on the counter near me. I picked it up and began cleaning it. I tried to appear brave and hold a conversation with him.

Mary taking a break.

"I suppose your husband is home," he said.

"Oh yes." He was in Greenland.

I was scared to death. He gave me a long look and seemed to be weighing his options. I never let go of the knife. He backed off, returned to the bar, finished his sandwich and left. My mother always worried about such situations. She told me I should keep the doors locked at night, but I explained to her that the customers wouldn't be able to get in if I did that. The restaurant was open until 1:00 in the morning, but when business was slow during the week, I sometimes closed up early.

Another time when I was alone, a trucker came in and had obviously had enough to drink somewhere else. I told him he would have to leave; I wouldn't serve him in the condition he was in. He didn't give me an argument about it, like I feared he might, and left. I watched out the north window as he headed his big rig up the highway, swerving all over. I didn't really want to get him in any trouble, but I also didn't want him killing himself or someone else, so I called the sheriff. When the paper came out, I read about a trucker getting picked up north of Randolph.

There were many other times when I had to refuse someone a drink. I ran a respectable establishment and didn't put up with things getting out of hand. Swearing was something I didn't care for and Bob wouldn't tolerate it. Once in awhile, he would tell someone to "hold their tongue." Bob always said, "Anybody that swears is ignorant."

I heard Bob swear only once in all the years I knew him. For the second morning in a row, he stubbed his bare toe on the metal leg of the bed. He said nothing the first time it happened, but I imagine stubbing an already sore and swollen toe is what caused him to utter the "God damn" I was so shocked to hear. I couldn't help myself, I laid in bed and laughed.

Seventeen

I knew if I were to ever have any real business, I
needed to serve more than soup and sandwiches.
We visited our friendly banker once again. With the
borrowed money, we purchased equipment to
upgrade the kitchen, with a small, stainless steel
dishwasher that did a load in three minutes flat
and deep fat fryers. Now I could expand the menu
to include French fries, onion rings, and golden,
deep fried chicken and fish.

I hired Ben Anklan to cook for me, Joe
DeAngelis to bartend and some good waitresses.
Ben was a great cook and very clean, which was

Mary and son John at the Lakeview Inn.

important to me. He had owned and operated a restaurant of his own at one time, in South St. Paul. The only thing I had to watch over with Ben was to make sure he was putting enough food on the plate. He was very tight with his portions. Whenever I reminded him to give bigger servings, he'd grumble that I was spoiling my customers.

Once a man and his family came in early in the evening to eat. None of my waitresses were in yet, so I waited on them. The man asked, "Say, is that Ben Anklan back there in the kitchen?" He could see him through the serving window.

"Yes, do you know him?"

"I used to eat at his restaurant in the cities."

When I brought their food, the gentleman remarked, "That's the most food I've ever seen Ben Anklan put on a plate!"

Every year, I applied for a hard liquor license and once the village finally voted it in, the Lakeview Inn became the first place in Randolph to ever have one. Eventually I got a Sunday liquor license, too.

Olie Davis ran the Polka Dot Tavern, a little joint on Highway 52, between Hampton and Cannon Falls. Her place was appropriately named; she had big, colored polka dots painted on the outside of the building.

Olie bootlegged, meaning she didn't have a liquor license but served it anyway. So when the state liquor agent came to check on me, I'd call up Olie. I never knew when he was coming, but it seemed he always hit my place first and headed in the direction of Olie's.

I'd say, "Hi Olie, I think you're going to have company soon," and she knew what I meant. A few days later she usually stopped in and I'd ask if she'd had her company. Sometimes the answer was yes, sometimes no, and she'd say,

"But I had my dishes done," which meant she had all the booze hidden.

The agents could close you down if you were caught. I would never have dared to bootleg, but many other bar owners did. I had too much at stake—my business and my boys.

Word spread and business picked up. My Friday night fish fries drew in a good crowd. In time, we were serving 90 to 100 customers every Friday. We had lots of regulars from all over. They were even coming down from the cities. Once in awhile, an out-of-towner stopped in wondering where the Lakeview Inn was. I would tell him he was in the right place, but that our sign blew away in a strong wind and we hadn't had a chance to put up a new one. We were well enough established by then, that we never did put up another sign.

Sometimes visitors wondered where the view of the lake was. I would point in the right direction and say, "Oh, if you squint, you can see it." Only people from out of town called the restaurant by its official name. Everybody else called the place "Mary's."

There were some people from the area who wouldn't come into my restaurant to eat because it was also a drinking establishment. I imagine my beer-battered chicken and fish were taboo, as well!

My Sunday special, baked chicken with dressing and mashed potatoes, was a real hit. I baked the halved chickens in a large, oiled pan in the oven, skin side down, with a scoop of homemade sage dressing on top. I made a tasty gravy from the flavorful brown drippings left in the pan, using water, flour, salt and pepper. I didn't use fancy herbs or seasonings and I had no special secrets, but everybody raved about my baked chicken dinner. After many years I got to the point of nearly throwing up every time I opened that oven door. I have a hard time stomaching chicken to this day.

Elaine Andrews was my first waitress, back when we initially opened. Over the years I had lots of good hired help: Joyce Chambers, Marilyn Koldstad, Shirley Kuhn, Ann Murray, Evelyn Brown, Helen Holte, Peg DeAngelis, Sheila Murray, and Jean Brunotte, to name a few. They made a dollar an hour, plus tips.

Bernie Bremer was my top girl. All my help was good and would do anything I asked of them, but Bernie did things without being asked. If it was slow and a window needed washing, Bernie washed the window. She was a hard worker and a mother of ten children besides. Being Native American, Bernie always called them her ten little Indians.

When things were slow, the girls and I took time for breaks to enjoy ourselves a little. We worked crossword puzzles, sang, told jokes and drank a few Grain Belts. Once all

Bernie Bremer and some of her clan, at the restaurant.

the customers were gone, Bernie and I, and sometimes Joyce or one of the other gals, sat and drank a few more, discussing issues about everybody and everything. It's surprising what you can accomplish over a glass of beer with a good friend. We solved many of the world's problems.

When the last of my help left, I always had one more beer after I'd gathered all the ashtrays and lined them up on the bar. I never dumped them in the trash until the next morning, when I knew for sure there were no live butts. I checked all the booths for dropped cigarettes, too. I couldn't sleep if I was worried about a fire starting.

So there I sat, behind the bar, relaxing my tired bones, with only the light from my cigarette piercing the darkness and the welcomed silence of an empty bar. I liked to watch the last of the traffic go by outside, as I summed up the evening's activities in my mind.

It was usually 2:00 in the morning before I got to bed, and I always had to be up by at least 10:00 a.m. That's when the weekly deliveries began arriving. On the day the meat man came with all my fresh meat, I made hamburger patties and re-cleaned all the chickens—another reason I don't care to eat chicken these days. Some of the meat I re-packaged and froze for later. That was always a big day.

When I needed bread and buns, I called an order in to the Hi-Quality Bakery in Cannon Falls and they delivered that same day. The vegetable man brought me all my produce—cabbage for Ben's delicious homemade coleslaw, bags of frozen French fries, salad fixings, and anything I needed for our family meals. I never went to the grocery store. Everything was delivered to my doorstep and we ate high off the hog.

The milkman came each week, as did the hard liquor salesman and the beer trucks from Old Style and Hamms.

Paul and Ole brought me all my Grain Belt, which is what I had on tap and was the biggest seller. That was my beer of choice. Bill Hoff, my cigarette man, kept me stocked with all the brands, along with gum and candy. Every day someone was busy unloading goods and I was busy writing them checks.

Bob and I didn't see much of each other. He was occupied with his own work and I with mine. Our schedules were so different, with me working late and him going to bed early. I packed lunches for Bob and the boys at night and kept them in the refrigerator. Bob often ate his breakfast at Little Oscars—a diner in Hampton—and Jim and John fixed themselves cereal and toast. The boys were good about doing their chores and getting themselves off to school.

I worked hard and was on my feet a lot, the twenty years I ran "Mary's." I was closed Mondays and Tuesdays. That gave me two days to scrub and wax floors, and make out and call in my orders, in addition to the everyday chores of cleaning our living quarters, doing the laundry and cooking meals for my family.

I used my own home-made soap to wash clothes, just as my mother did. She used hog fat to make hers, but I had the fat from the deep fryer to make mine with. I mixed the fat with a can of lye and heated it together in a big shallow pan. I left it to cool, then cut it into bars. When I did the wash, I used a cheese grater to shave off pieces into the machine. It didn't always dissolve completely and sometimes we found little chunks of soap on our clothes.

Each time the health inspector came, he always said I ran a "clean ship," and I knew I did. My mother had raised me that way.

Eighteen

My sons grew, before my business did. They were handsome young men. Jim started seeing a gal, Judy Stave from Cannon Falls. I could tell things were getting serious, the way he talked about this cute car-hop that waited on him at the Cannon Drive-In.

In the spring of '57, just as Jim was turning eighteen and graduating from high school, I learned he was going to become a father.

There was some sort of falling out between the young couple, and Jim left for the summer to help his uncles down on the farm. Maybe he just needed time to sort things out.

John.   *Jim.*

When I told Bob he was going to be a grandpa he asked, "How can that be?" I don't think he could comprehend what I was telling him, but once it sunk in, he didn't have much to say, as usual.

On Bob's fiftieth birthday our first grandchild was born, a baby girl. I had Bob take me to the hospital in Red Wing in hopes of seeing her, but the hospital staff wouldn't let me in. I left in tears, wondering if I would ever see her.

Thank Heaven, things worked out in the end, and Jim and Judy made their amends. They were married the following summer and my granddaughter Teri was a joy to have in my life. Jim and Judy went on to bless me with four more grandchildren, Tami, Robby, Ritchie and Randy.

John also married and he and Gerry added three more to my list of grandkids, Dan, Lynette and Janel. The grandchildren have grown up, married and have children of their own, making me a great-grandmother a dozen times. I love them all dearly.

⟨⬦⟩────

Grandma Mary with Teri.

As is the balance of life, along with the happy times of birth, there comes the sadness of death.

My 81-year-old mother was still down on the farm with John, late in the fall of 1958. John was concerned about mother and called to keep me updated. She was really beginning to lose it. When he left the house to do chores, he told her to wave a white dishtowel if she needed him. He would no more than get out to the barn and there she was, waving the towel. He couldn't get much accomplished the way things were going.

She was getting more confused all along. As soon as breakfast was over, she started making lunch. John said the potatoes were fried to a crisp by the time he came in to eat.

Her condition worsened, and in January I received a call from John, telling me I better come. Mom was in the hospital. Judy, Teri and I went down. Jim was in the Navy at the time, stationed in California, and Judy and Teri were living with us.

While I was in her hospital room, one of the nurses was putting a board on the side of her bed to keep her in. Earlier, she had been running up and down the halls, calling for John. She looked at me now, and said, "He's putting that up to keep the pigs out." I knew then that she was off her rocker.

John and I discussed it and thought it best I take her home to live with me. The doctors had her all doped up and said we were foolish for wanting to take her home with us. A nurse said, "I don't envy you."

We took Mom out of the hospital and back to the farm to pack her things. Mom was in the back seat of the car and as I pulled out of the driveway and headed up the road, I looked in the rearview mirror. She was looking out through the back window at the farm, her home, her life. Sadly, I thought to myself, she will never see this place again. And she didn't.

Once back at home with me and off all the medication they had her on, she perked up some and most of the time she seemed to be her old self. At times, she was confused, so I would put her on the right track and then she seemed all right for a awhile. In conversation, she'd say, "When I get back home…" She worried about John and talked about him often. Two days before she died, she wrote a letter to him.

Randolph, Minn.
Mar 27,/59

    Dear John. I am sorry I didn't write you last week but I wasn't a bit well. Am feeling better today. I am almost counting the days till I will see you. Some times I think maybe you don't want to be bothered with me. Then again I know I've done the best I could remembering you have done everything to make me comfortable and I am so very happy that I have children thats so considerate of me and do everything for me. I am sure there isn't many as comfortable as I am.

    If I've failed you I am sorry. Please over look all mistakes. I am so glad you could help Irene. She has been so good to us all. Maybe we can give her a lift some time. I am glad she feels she can be one of us. We are proud to have her as one of the family. You can see how I try to write and make a mess of it. You drop me a line anytime and I not neglect to write you.

              Love to every one of all
                Write. Lena/Mother

It was the Saturday morning before Easter when I brought her a half of a grapefruit for breakfast. After she ate, she asked me to help her to the bathroom. Just as I got her up, everything came from inside her and she fell back on the bed. I knew the end was near. I recalled a similar time, so long ago, with Sadie. I called Doc Williams right away and he in turn called the hospital. I woke up my son, John, and had him ride in the ambulance with Mother. I couldn't leave, I had Teri to watch. I called Judy at the National Tea—the grocery store in Cannon Falls where she worked—explained the situation and asked her to pick up John and bring him home. I then called my brother John. My mind was in a fog, my heart was heavy and I prayed this wasn't happening.

Bernie Bremer took me to the hospital later and I sat with Mom awhile, but she didn't rally at all. I went back home to anxiously wait for John. He pulled in about 3:00 in the morning, weary from the eight-hour drive by himself and the worry that he wouldn't get here in time to see Mom alive. It was a sleepless night.

At 7:00 the next morning, the hospital called and said we had better come. My brother John, Bob and I went down right away. Once there, they said we should get the minister, so Bob went to the Stanton Church to round him up. After the minister was done preaching on Easter morning he came to give Lena her last blessings.

Just as he said a final prayer, the sun streaming in through the window brightened, touching my mother's face and she took her final breath. I stood there, numb.

A few days later, I tearfully boarded the train in Northfield, escorting my mother's body on her final train trip. We laid her to rest next to my father. It was one of the saddest times in my life. A great lady was gone.

*Lena Gilson
7/10/1877–
3/29/1959.*

$\mathcal{E}$pilogue

I felt it fitting to end the words of my grandma here, at the birth of her first grandchild—me—and at the death of her beloved mother, my great-grandmother, Lena Gilson.

Grandma stayed on in the restaurant business until 1969. My great-grandfather, James Ferguson, Sr., built the station he talked about, in 1961, next door to the restaurant, for his grandsons to run. My dad, Jim, worked there with his brother, my uncle John, for awhile, but there wasn't enough money in it to support our growing family. That was in the days when gas was 25.9 cents a gallon and an oil change was $5.00, and that included washing the windows, inside and out, a vacuum and a dust.

Lakeview Inn and John's Conoco, 1962.

The lake home in 1959.

My dad went on to become a welder with the Boilermakers Union. John sold the station in 1963 and became an electrician. Both did very well for themselves and were respected men in their trades.

Grandpa Bob worked for the University of Minnesota at a research facility in Rosemount, as head of general maintenance, from 1958 until 1973. He and my grandma moved to Arizona and spent two winters, after their retirement, but eventually returned to their home on Lake Byllesby, a little house with knotty pine walls and a beautiful stone fireplace. Tony Kruze, my grandpa and my great-grandpa Jim built the cozy house in 1958, and Great-Grandpa Jim lived there until he sold it to my grandparents in 1963. At that time, since my grandparents were still in the restaurant, my parents and we kids lived there for the next six years, until Grandma retired.

In late October 1972, the Rendezvous—formerly the Lakeview Inn—was completely destroyed by a fire which broke out in the middle of the night. My dad was among the volunteer firemen who fought to extinguish the horrendous blaze. I'll never forget standing in our yard looking out across the field watching the flames in sad disbelief.

In 1983, Grandpa Bob, Uncle John, and my dad took a train out West to Seattle for a special reunion. Bob Foster's daughter had arranged for her dad to reunite with his biological father and meet his half brothers for the first time. My dad and uncle made three more trips, over the years, to see their brother Bob, and he made the trip to Minnesota a few times. All four men were happy to get to know each other after all those years.

Grandma and Grandpa celebrated their 50th wedding anniversary at the lake in 1984, with family and friends.

Grandpa suffered a stroke in 1986, and Grandma cared for him in their home until his death in October of that same year. Grandpa's death was hard on Grandma, she felt

The lake home in 1993.

she would lose her mind. A year after Grandpa's death, Grandma forced herself to move on with her life and began to see the world. She felt guilty about spending money at first, but soon realized that keeping busy kept her mind off of her sadness. In the past fifteen years, she has enjoyed traveling to all fifty states and seven other countries.

Grandma still resides at the lake, enjoying the beauty of the water and cliffs, thankful for what she considers the most beautiful spot on the lake. She loves her flowers, the birds, and the sunsets. Every Friday she drives herself four miles to Cannon Falls, to play Bridge. She's witty and forgetful and I love her.

I'm so thankful for her story, for saving letters, pictures and diaries, and for sharing it all with me. My father was a huge help also. What Grandma couldn't remember, he did. He encouraged and supported me through it all. I asked them hundreds of questions, took thousands of notes, and we all spent valuable time together.

In May, 2002, the three of us took a trip to Iowa. My grandma hadn't been there since 1995, when she went down for her brother Phil's funeral. We stayed three days, visiting cemeteries, going to the Milner farm, the Bayles farm and the Gilson farm, (places she hadn't visited for many, many years), uncovering family records in the Mount Pleasant library and speaking with lots of people. We even drove to Clarion, where Grandma was born. The last time she was there was over eighty years ago. During our trip, I wrote in my journal…

I think the Gilson angels were with us today and yesterday as we traveled through the countryside of southern Iowa. As I witnessed my dad and my grandma travel back to the old Iowa in their minds, I felt the presence of Lena, Guy, Phil, Joe and John. The path was cleared and our way made easy because they wanted us here. They welcomed our presence and our purpose.

All the people we have met have been so friendly, willing to tell us anything they knew, sharing their memories with honesty. Everyone we encountered remembered the family members we wanted to know about. They all seemed glad to travel with us backward in time and remember the faces and the places and speak those names they hadn't thought about in years.

Many times in the past, Dad has gone by the farm, but the gate was always locked and no one around. Today the gate was open and Jim Turner, the 85 year old man who bought the place from John in '67, was there. How fortunate we felt to drive right up to the house (although the original house is gone), and walk the grounds, take pictures and talk to him.

Everyone we met had something new to share, shed light on things we were in the dark about, or led us to someone else who could do more of the same. It's been marvelous. And to see Dad and Grandma reminisce and enjoy this venture has been so heartwarming.

Phil Gilson lived on the farm with his mother and brother John from the time of his divorce from Carolyn, until he remarried in 1958, to a lady by the name of Irene Willits. They lived close to the Gilson farm for many years. Irene passed away in 1993 and Phil two years later. They are buried in the Maple Hill Cemetery in VanBuren County, just east of Birmingham. Phil never associated much with his relatives in Minnesota after he got married the second time. I

remember once, when my family went to Iowa, we stopped
in at Phil's and Irene's house. It wasn't much of a place, old
and run down and Phil didn't have much to say. I never
really knew him, not like I knew my great-uncle John. Uncle
John was always fun to be around. My family looked forward
to his visits up our way and to our visits down to Iowa.

John Gilson continued to live in the old farmhouse by
himself after Lena died, farming the land and doing electrical
work in the area. He closed off the upstairs of the house, the
back bedroom and the kitchen. He moved the refrigerator
and sink into the living room and cooked on a hot plate.
After each meal he'd wipe his plate clean with a piece of
bread so he didn't have to do dishes. He used to go down to
the creek to take a bath and wash his clothes. The old Jungers
oil stove kept the two rooms he lived in warm and cozy, and
he lived that way for a number of years.

Most of John's neighbors were elderly, some had never
married, and those that had, never had any children. John
took care of them all. If someone needed help, needed something done, John always worked it in some way. He was so
good-hearted and they all loved and depended on John.

Every noon he went into the little town of Lockridge for
lunch. Katie Zihlman had an upholstery shop in the basement of the café where John ate. The two met and formed a
friendship and a business partnership. John was handy and
he loved working with wood, so he helped Katie, refinishing
furniture part-time.

John bought an old abandoned café in town and turned
the building into an upholstery shop that he and Katie ran,
with a small area in the back for living quarters, where John
lived after he sold the farm. Right behind the shop was a little house that used to be the office from the old lumber yard,

which had gone out of business. John bought that place, too, and Katie lived there.

On November 21st, 1970, John, at the age of 59, married Katie at the 1st Augustana Lutheran Church in town. They enjoyed sixteen years of married life together, and were a fun and entertaining couple. John died on May 31, 1986, after suffering from emphysema. Katie was laid to rest next to him, in Grant Cemetery after her death on October 12th, 1996, the same cemetery in Rome where my great, great-grandparents, Lemuel and Rebecca are buried, along with their son Frank, my great-grandparents, Guy and Lena, and Joe, three generations of Gilsons.

Since I began this project, I have learned things I never knew. I now know people I never met, and I tell their story. The people I've written about were not wealthy, highly educated, or famous. But they were real people that lived their lives with dignity, compassion and love for one another. They were strong, hard-working, humble individuals—people that deserve to be recognized and remembered. I hope to honor and preserve their memory with this book.

To gather more information about Grandma, I wrote to a couple of old friends of hers, asking them to share any memories they might have. Here are two of the responses - the first from Joyce Chambers, a good friend and former waitress at the Lakeview Inn.

Hi Teri,

I think it is wonderful you're writing a book about Grandma's life and hope I can read it someday. I have been thinking about the years past, wondering really how much I can remember that you can use. I remember them being one of the first people we met when we moved to Randolph in 1945. There is about 18 years difference in our age, so never knew her real well, until I started working for her in her restaurant. She was a great lady to work for, and a very clean, fussy person but pleasant to work with. The three of us (Mary, Bernie Bremer and myself) worked together well. When we had a little break between crowds, Mary would say, " time for a little Scotch tea" and we would sit and drink some beer. After closing and the work was done, more "Scotch tea!" On Saturday night we would get ready for her famous baked chicken and dressing special served only on Sundays!

She and Dale (my husband) worked the crossword puzzles in the Sunday paper. They sometimes got together to compare answers.

When the FDA would inspect her restaurant, they would tell her she ran a "clean ship!"

I can't ever remember her having any trouble with anybody at the bar. She could handle them well with a few words and a "look." We always called it her "eagle eye." Everyone seemed to respect her very well. She managed a nice, clean restaurant with a quiet atmosphere and soft music in the background.

One Halloween we dressed up and went bar-hopping. Mary and Bertie Charlton dressed as clowns! Was a fun time! Always a good time with Grandma Mary!

I remember an election one year in our small town - don't remember just who was on the ballot but he was not too popular, but your Grandpa liked him and Grandma didn't but she thought if he only got one vote, then Grandpa would know she didn't vote for him. I think he got 4 or 5 so we laughed about it and said she wouldn't have had to vote for him!

*When your Grandpa died, she put one of his slippers
filled with flowers on his grave. I thought it was very
touching.*

*She always liked to have me come and sit on her
patio and visit too. She does love the lake and her home.
I never heard anything but good about your Grandma
and I am proud to be one of her friends.*

As ever,

Joyce

This letter from her long time friend, Dell Rambo
Morrill...

Dear Teri,

*Where do I begin to tell you about my friendship
with "old friend Mary," your grandmother?*

*We first met in 1927 when we were in 7th grade. My
family moved to Randolph from New Hampton, Iowa. My
dad transferred to work on the C.G.W. Railroad.*

*Needless to say, we have remained best friends
through all the years since then. That's 79 years.*

*Mary and Bob were married in November, 1934,
the year we graduated from high school. Bob was gone
all week at his job in Red Wing. That left Mary all
alone in that big house on the hill. I stayed nights with
her during the week. I'll always remember that wonderful home-made bread Mary toasted for breakfast. She
sent me off to my work at school with a full tummy.*

*Clair and I married in 1938. We were best friends
with Bob and Mary. The guys had flying for a common
interest. We girls were weekend flying "widows." Mary*

had a tavern on the main drag in Randolph and later
one in the basement of the hotel. We called the basement one "the blue room" because everyone smoked and
ventilation was poor. Of course, it was a gathering place
for all of us. We had good times there.

The twins, your dad and John, were born in 1939,
our son Denny in 1940 and Jeff in 1943. Mary and I
had a lot of fun—and trials—raising our boys. We
finally got them grown up. In spite of the mischief they
got into, they grew up to be good citizens. When they
were little, the guys gave Mary and me a night out once
a week while they babysat. They had their night out
(sometimes more than one). We usually got sitters on
Saturday and all went out for a night of fun.

Mary opened her supper club on highway 56. I can
still taste the delicious chicken, mashed potatoes and
gravy special. Her Friday night fish fry was super good
and always drew lots of eaters. Food was Mary's talent.
She served the best!! (Still does)

I could tell Mary anything and knew it would never
be repeated. That's truly a real friend. In all the 79
years we've been friends, I can't think of a time we ever
had an argument or a cross word.

To sum it up, I love your grandmother dearly. She is
the best friend I've ever had and probably will never find
another like her. We've had a lot of fun together and
shared some not so good times.

I've rambled on and still haven't covered all that we
did. I hope you can filter out some of this to use in your
book.

I'm enclosing a poem Mary sent me after I had rectal surgery in 1974-75. She wrote some good poetry. Another one of her talents!

Love,
Dell

Grandma sent her a little card she made with a picture of a women's behind (in underwear) on the cover with the words—*'The Butt of the Matter'*
Inside the card it reads...

You got problems with the rear.
Oh my gosh you poor dear.
They cut you up and cut you down
And cut you all the way around.
I bet you knew from the start
You'd never by able to let a _____.
You better come up here by the lake
And let me tend you, for goodness sake.
We will listen to the meadow lark
And take long walks in the park.
I bet by this time Dell
You feel you've really gone through Hell.
And now I must say farewell.

Your old pal,
Mary

Another one of the many poems my Grandma wrote, this one to my Grandpa in 1974, on their wedding anniversary...

It's forty years ago today
You promised me you would obey.
I really thought you meant those words,
But soon found out they were for the birds.
My thoughts of running away were strong.
But then the kids, they came along.
Clouds would gather like a storm,
But they always cleared by early morn.
After forty years of wedded bliss
I sit down and reminisce.
Remember when you stole that kiss?
You wrote me love letters in the sand
And promised me that wedding band.
You called me your 'turtle dove'
And said I was your only love.
Then suddenly your hair grew thin
And I grew another chin.
You looked at me and I looked at you.
We couldn't believe that it was true.
If we don't make another year, we won't care
We have had our share
Of ups and downs, like merry-go-rounds.

I wanted to send a letter to Bernie Bremer, like I had to Dell and Joyce, to get her memories of Grandma. They hadn't seen each other for many years, but Grandma knew she had moved out to South Dakota long ago. I called one of Bernie's daughters to get the address and found out Bernie was in town visiting with another daughter. We couldn't believe our luck, here she was just a few miles away. We called immediately and set up a day to meet.

I picked Bernie up the following week. She doesn't get around too easily, but I got her to Grandma's house and it was worth it. This was some of the conversation...

Me: Bernie, what do you remember about working for Grandma?

Bernie: I got a dollar an hour, good tips and all the beer I could drink. We worked crosswords, sang and told jokes. Bob would get sick and tired of us and go in the other room and shut the door.

Grandma: Bernie cooked for him one night. When she served it to him, he said, "What's that?" Bernie told him, "It's Kosher, eat it." Bob always liked Bernie.

Bernie: He said I was a lady.

Grandma: You two talked the same language.

Me: What's the secret to your longevity?

Bernie: We drank beer (They both giggle) and we loved each other.

Grandma: We're the only ones left breathing.

Bernie: And I'm barely!

I later wrote my observations...

To witness today, the reunion of two old friends, both in their eighties, Bernie Bremer and Mary Ferguson, was special. I'll never forget them hugging with Bernie's oxygen tank between them. To see them sitting side by side on the couch, reminiscing after all these years, was precious.

I noticed they both have these beautiful, old hands, with long slender fingers. When I brought this to their attention, they held hands and admired one another's. Grandma told Bernie how much she liked her Black Hills gold ring. Bernie stroked Grandma's thin, aged skin and took in every detail, commenting on how dainty Grandma's hands have always been, that she has never forgotten those hands. Grandma's comment was how much work their hands had seen over the years. Bernie agreed wholeheartedly.

When it was time to go, Bernie and Grandma gave each other a long, sincere hug. Grandma said, "You were my best waitress."

Bernie said, "You were my best friend. I love you."

"Oh, Bernie, I love you, too," Grandma said.

As we went out the door, Bernie waved, "Bye, bye honey" It was the sweetest thing. I was so glad I was able to bring these two 'old gals' back together.

John Ferguson Remembers...

I recall a summer I spent down on the farm to help Uncle John. On Saturday nights we took the eggs up to Four Corners to sell and then bought a few groceries for the week. The old country store, run by the Smithbergs, didn't have a big stock of inventory, but we bought things like flour and sugar. Lena always liked visiting with Mrs. Smithberg; they were good friends. The pot belly stove in the middle of the store, with tables around it, was where the men sat and played Euchre.

As payment for helping Uncle John that summer, he took me back home and bought me a brand new, green three-speed bike at the Coast to Coast in Cannon Falls. It cost $52.00.

I remember a time when Jim and I were about eight years old and down on the farm. Uncle John had run over one of the cats with the tractor, so Jim and I dug a hole and buried the cat. As we stomped on the grave to pack down the dirt, we heard "meow." We looked at each other, wide-eyed, quick dug up the grave, and I hit the cat over the head as hard as I could. I know now it was just the voice box being compressed that made the loud meow.

John wasn't too happy I broke the handle on his new shovel trying to kill a dead cat.

Another memory at the farm, that could have had a far worse ending than it did, was the time Jim and I were helping Uncle John load hay from the barn into the back of the pickup. Jim and I had a deal worked out—I would open the gate going in and Jim had to open the gate going out. We got our load, but when it was time to leave, I looked around, and no Jim to open the gate. "I don't know where he is," I said disgusted, as I threw the pitchfork in the hay. Out popped Jim in a hurry from his hiding place, beneath the hay. I had caught him in the leg with the sharp tines of the pitchfork.

When we were living at the Gilson house, Jim and I would wait for Uncle Joe to come in on the train on Fridays. He used to come down from the cities to Randolph and stay on weekends. When he got there, he always played ball with us. One time, Uncle Joe said I could bat first, which made Jim mad, so when it was his turn to bat, I pitched the ball, but instead of trying to hit it, Jim threw the bat directly at me. I couldn't duck fast enough and it hit me right in the nose. It bled terrible. Uncle Joe spanked Jim that day, but he had to chase him around the yard and through the evergreens to catch him first.

Jim Ferguson Remembers...

I'm especially fond of my memories of the trains. I always looked forward to a train ride when I was a kid. John and I traveled by ourselves sometimes and the railroad employees took good care of us. The porter would come by and ask if we wanted a pillow.

I loved looking out the window at the scenery. The feel of the train was so relaxing, the swaying of the cars back and forth. When it got dark, I'd doze off, but I was wide awake as soon as we got to a town. I especially loved coming into a town at night, with all the lights and activity, the train passing in front of the cars as they waited at the crossing.

The blow of the train's whistle was louder when we were in town, the sound echoing off the buildings. There were so many sounds I loved about the train. I'd lay back, close my eyes and listen to it all...the ding-ding-ding of the bells as the cross arms went up or down, the hum of the people's conversations around me, the clickety-clack as the train went over the joints of the track. I can still hear the voice of the conductor as he came through and hollered "Lockridge, thirty minutes" or "all aboard." But mostly, I loved (and still do) the sound of the train's whistle.

I remember the dining car with its fine linens and guys sitting around smoking cigars in the smoker car. As I walked through the train, the noise from the track was much louder in between the cars. In the winter it was really cold walking through there.

The railroad hired detectives to keep bums off the trains. Railroad Dicks, they were called, and although they were undercover, you could usually pick them out. They wore the nicer suits. They also carried a hidden club and they would get tough if they caught someone doing something wrong.

There was a hobo camp at the cascades in Randolph. The bums traveled as stowaways on the trains, staying for the summer, working odd jobs, weeding gardens and mowing grass. They used to put a mark of some sort on a sign post or tree to show where there was an easy place to get food. I'm sure they had the Gilson house marked when my Grandma lived there.

Our parents warned us not to get too friendly with the bums. One time, down at the pit, where us kids used to swim, one of the bums caught a turtle. He told each of us to bring some food the next day, potatoes, carrots, crackers, or whatever we could find in the garden or sneak from the cupboards. "Tomorrow we'll have turtle stew," he said. The next day we all showed up with something and he cooked it all together over an open fire. We enjoyed our lunch with him, but never told our folks.

My parents also warned me not to crawl under the trains. You never knew for sure if the train was going to back up or go forward, so I always crawled under in the middle, away from the wheels. It was the freight trains that were always sitting there, blocking our way, and they were slower to take off, so it didn't seem that dangerous to me. I knew ahead of time when the box car was about to move, because I could hear the couplers start clanking at the head of the train and the sound working its way down as each car was jerked forward, a chain reaction of each coupler tightening up. The longer the train, the louder the clang, especially by the time it got to the caboose.

I never crawled under at the crossing, for someone was sure to see me there. Sometimes I used the steps where two cars connected. That was a safer way to get from one side to the other.

I don't remember much about Grandpa Gilson, because I was so young when he died, but I certainly remember my grandma. The first thing that comes to mind is what a funny lady she was, so witty. And she loved to socialize. Down on the farm, they had about eight people on their phone line, a party line they called it. Everyone had their own ring, like two shorts and a long. They all knew their own ring, of course, and also knew everyone else's. So if a person was curious to know who was calling their neighbor, they just quietly picked up and listened. They referred to this as rubbering. This happened often and Lena's neighbors not only rubbered on her while she was talking, but she rubbered in on them from time to time, too.

Grandma always wore a full apron and it served many purposes, like gathering fruit from the trees and vegetables from the garden. She could carry a lot in her apron.

I remember Uncle Phil helped with the farming when he wasn't busy running the maintainer. When he was up on the tractor, he had to swing his wooden leg up over the steering wheel in order to get off. He always walked with a limp, but he got along well with his artificial leg, and he could even run.

Once, when I was a kid, I was giving him a hard time about something and he took off after me. He never did catch me, but I sure was surprised at how fast he could go.

Uncle John was a great guy. He and I were very close and had so many good times together. I'll never forget one weekend when I went down to see him, it was probably in the mid sixties, when he was just living in two rooms. I got down there late on a Friday night and we stayed up for hours, talking, laughing and reminiscing. In the morning, when John got up to do chores, I told him I would fix us some breakfast. When he came in to eat, we sat down to a hot meal of eggs, bacon and toast. As we ate, I commented that the bacon was so dark and the eggs kind of were too.

He said, "Ya, I noticed that. What did you cook them in?"

"The frying pan that was in the sink."

"Oh, God, the dog ate out of that last night!"

"Gee, it looked clean."

"Ya, Gus was hungry."

We laughed so hard we could barely finish our black breakfast. We did eat it all, though; we figured the germs got killed in the cooking process. John and I laughed about it for years after that, every time we got together, it was brought up.

He died the same year as my dad and they are the two people I miss the most in my life.

Grandma

I love your stories
of days gone by.
They make me laugh
and sometimes cry.

I learn and grow from
these stories told.
Of when you were young
in the days of old.

I watch the distant,
look in your eye,
as you talk of those days
and smile and sigh.

In your voice I hear love
for those years you knew.
The people, the places
that are a part of you.

Your life has spanned
many a year,
your memories of them
seem so dear.

Each day may not have
always been bright,
But from this you've grown
and gained insight.

And from that insight
you pass on to me
wisdom and truth,
so a better person I'll be.

Hold on to those memories
and continue to share.
I'll never stop listening,
I'll always be there.

HAPPY 82ND BIRTHDAY
LOVE, TERI

Written in 1996

An Interview with Grandma Mary

What's your favorite…?
   Color—"Blue"
   Food—"Steak"
   Game—"Bridge"
   Place—"By the lake"
   Vacation—"When Tami and I went to
      Switzerland."

Memory—"When you kids were small and I
   would come visit you down at the lake. I
   would walk in and hear 'Grandma's here,
   Grandma's here!' and you would all come
   crawling out of the basement."

What was the happiest day of your life? "When
   I was going with Bob, and even though he
   was so timid, he reached over and kissed me
   and told me he loved me."

What makes you cry? "News of the war that's
   going on now. I listen to it because I want
   to know what's going on, but I cry."

Any regrets? "Yes, that we ever moved to
   Arizona. We gave up so much at the lake.

I had it fixed up the way I wanted. Then we came back to an empty house and had to start over. That was a bad time for me. I've regretted that so much, selling beautiful stuff I couldn't replace. It was really worse for Bob's health, moving out there."

Did you ever regret marrying Grandpa? "Yes, many times in the past I have regretted it. When we were courting, he was so attentive, so loving. Once we were married, everything changed. It was as though he thought, 'I've got her caged now, she can't get away,' and he went about his own business, forgetting about me. We never had a good, strong relationship after that. But now, looking back, I'm not sorry we had a life together, even though we had rocky times, as many couples do. I don't think I would have been better off without him. I loved Bob and he loved me. He was a good, honest man."

What is your greatest accomplishment? "I've never done anything that's an accomplishment. Jim and John turned out very good, though. I've always been proud of my kids."

Don't you consider running a successful business something to be proud of, too? "No. I just knew I had a job to do and I did it. I hoped I was doing it right. I made a lot of mistakes, but they were honest mistakes."

How do you hope people remember you? "I've always tried to be kind to people and help them if I could. I hope they remember me as kind."

Mary at her lake home, 2002.

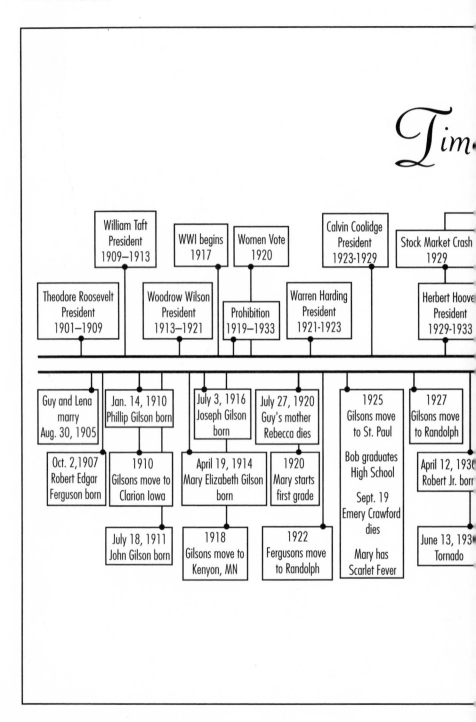

Tim

William Taft
President
1909–1913

WWI begins
1917

Women Vote
1920

Calvin Coolidge
President
1923-1929

Stock Market Crash
1929

Theodore Roosevelt
President
1901–1909

Woodrow Wilson
President
1913–1921

Prohibition
1919–1933

Warren Harding
President
1921-1923

Herbert Hoove
President
1929-1933

Guy and Lena
marry
Aug. 30, 1905

Jan. 14, 1910
Phillip Gilson born

July 3, 1916
Joseph Gilson
born

July 27, 1920
Guy's mother
Rebecca dies

1925
Gilsons move
to St. Paul

Bob graduates
High School

Sept. 19
Emery Crawford
dies

Mary has
Scarlet Fever

1927
Gilsons move
to Randolph

Oct. 2,1907
Robert Edgar
Ferguson born

1910
Gilsons move to
Clarion Iowa

April 19, 1914
Mary Elizabeth Gilson
born

1920
Mary starts
first grade

April 12, 1930
Robert Jr. bor

July 18, 1911
John Gilson born

1918
Gilsons move to
Kenyon, MN

1922
Fergusons move
to Randolph

June 13, 193
Tornado

Line

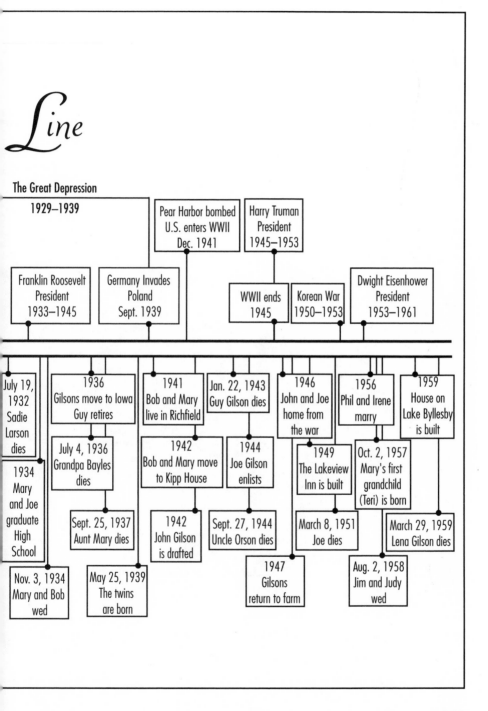

The Great Depression
1929–1939

Pear Harbor bombed
U.S. enters WWII
Dec. 1941

Harry Truman
President
1945–1953

Franklin Roosevelt
President
1933–1945

Germany Invades
Poland
Sept. 1939

WWII ends
1945

Korean War
1950–1953

Dwight Eisenhower
President
1953–1961

July 19,
1932
Sadie
Larson
dies

1936
Gilsons move to Iowa
Guy retires

1941
Bob and Mary
live in Richfield

Jan. 22, 1943
Guy Gilson dies

1946
John and Joe
home from
the war

1956
Phil and Irene
marry

1959
House on
Lake Byllesby
is built

July 4, 1936
Grandpa Bayles
dies

1942
Bob and Mary move
to Kipp House

1944
Joe Gilson
enlists

1949
The Lakeview
Inn is built

Oct. 2, 1957
Mary's first
grandchild
(Teri) is born

1934
Mary
and Joe
graduate
High
School

Sept. 25, 1937
Aunt Mary dies

1942
John Gilson
is drafted

Sept. 27, 1944
Uncle Orson dies

March 8, 1951
Joe dies

March 29, 1959
Lena Gilson dies

Nov. 3, 1934
Mary and Bob
wed

May 25, 1939
The twins
are born

1947
Gilsons
return to farm

Aug. 2, 1958
Jim and Judy
wed

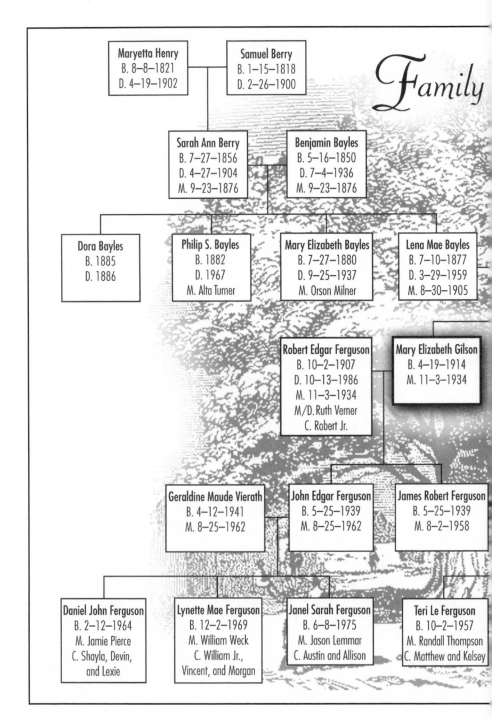

Family

Maryetta Henry
B. 8–8–1821
D. 4–19–1902

Samuel Berry
B. 1–15–1818
D. 2–26–1900

Sarah Ann Berry
B. 7–27–1856
D. 4–27–1904
M. 9–23–1876

Benjamin Bayles
B. 5–16–1850
D. 7–4–1936
M. 9–23–1876

Dora Bayles
B. 1885
D. 1886

Philip S. Bayles
B. 1882
D. 1967
M. Alta Turner

Mary Elizabeth Bayles
B. 7–27–1880
D. 9–25–1937
M. Orson Milner

Lena Mae Bayles
B. 7–10–1877
D. 3–29–1959
M. 8–30–1905

Robert Edgar Ferguson
B. 10–2–1907
D. 10–13–1986
M. 11–3–1934
M/D. Ruth Verner
C. Robert Jr.

Mary Elizabeth Gilson
B. 4–19–1914
M. 11–3–1934

Geraldine Maude Vierath
B. 4–12–1941
M. 8–25–1962

John Edgar Ferguson
B. 5–25–1939
M. 8–25–1962

James Robert Ferguson
B. 5–25–1939
M. 8–2–1958

Daniel John Ferguson
B. 2–12–1964
M. Jamie Pierce
C. Shayla, Devin,
and Lexie

Lynette Mae Ferguson
B. 12–2–1969
M. William Weck
C. William Jr.,
Vincent, and Morgan

Janel Sarah Ferguson
B. 6–8–1975
M. Jason Lemmar
C. Austin and Allison

Teri Le Ferguson
B. 10–2–1957
M. Randall Thompson
C. Matthew and Kelsey

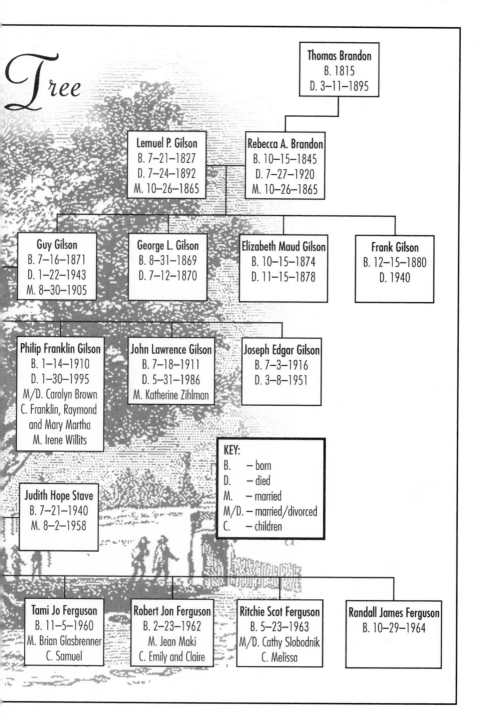

Tree

Thomas Brandon
B. 1815
D. 3–11–1895

Lemuel P. Gilson
B. 7–21–1827
D. 7–24–1892
M. 10–26–1865

Rebecca A. Brandon
B. 10–15–1845
D. 7–27–1920
M. 10–26–1865

Guy Gilson
B. 7–16–1871
D. 1–22–1943
M. 8–30–1905

George L. Gilson
B. 8–31–1869
D. 7–12–1870

Elizabeth Maud Gilson
B. 10–15–1874
D. 11–15–1878

Frank Gilson
B. 12–15–1880
D. 1940

Philip Franklin Gilson
B. 1–14–1910
D. 1–30–1995
M/D. Carolyn Brown
C. Franklin, Raymond
and Mary Martha
M. Irene Willits

John Lawrence Gilson
B. 7–18–1911
D. 5–31–1986
M. Katherine Zihlman

Joseph Edgar Gilson
B. 7–3–1916
D. 3–8–1951

KEY:
B. — born
D. — died
M. — married
M/D. — married/divorced
C. — children

Judith Hope Stave
B. 7–21–1940
M. 8–2–1958

Tami Jo Ferguson
B. 11–5–1960
M. Brian Glasbrenner
C. Samuel

Robert Jon Ferguson
B. 2–23–1962
M. Jean Maki
C. Emily and Claire

Ritchie Scot Ferguson
B. 5–23–1963
M/D. Cathy Slobodnik
C. Melissa

Randall James Ferguson
B. 10–29–1964